Scapegoats, Shambles & Shibboleths

# SCAPEGOATS, SHAMBLES & SHIBBOLETHS

## Martin H. Manser

Associate Editor: Andrew Bianchi

HODDER &
STOUGHTON

First published in Great Britain in 2009 by Hodder & Stoughton
An Hachette UK company

Visit the author's website: www.martinmanser.com

A CIP catalogue record for this title is available from the British Library.

ISBN 978 0 340 97979 2

Typeset in Filosofia by Ellipsis Books Limited

Printed and bound in Great Britain by
Clays Ltd, St Ives plc

Hodder & Stoughton policy is to use papers that are natural, renewable
and recyclable products and made from wood grown in sustainable forests.
The logging and manufacturing processes are expected to conform
to the environmental regulations of the country of origin.

Hodder & Stoughton Ltd
338 Euston Road
London NW1 3BH

www.hodderfaith.com

# Contents

# Introduction

They're *the salt of the earth*. He's a real *Good Samaritan*.
She's the *apple of his eye*. These are a few examples of
expressions from the Bible that have become well established in the English language. We use such phrases in
everyday speech, often without realising that they come
from the Bible. We also allude to biblical stories when
we say that *the writing is on the wall* when there are
ominous signs of an impending disaster, or when we
refer to someone returning like the *prodigal son*. At times
we even misquote the Bible when we say that *money is
the root of all evil*.

Such phrases all have their roots in the King James
(Authorised) Version of the Bible, published in 1611.
Since then, the English language has changed significantly and so this volume also includes a selection of
words that have their origin in older versions of the Bible
(e.g. *scapegoat*), or whose meanings have changed significantly since the seventeenth century (for example, *gin*,
*peculiar*, *shambles*).

An appendix lists some familiar phrases from the *Book*

*of Common Prayer* that have become part of the English language.

We have written this book to sketch the origin and development of a selection of biblical words and phrases in a way that we hope you will find not only entertaining but also informative.

Martin H. Manser
Andrew Bianchi

# A

## Abraham's bosom

*And it came to pass, that the beggar died, and was carried by the angels into Abraham's bosom: the rich man also died, and was buried.*

Luke 16:22

In this parable comparing the apathy of a rich man to the plight of an impoverished beggar called Lazarus in Luke 16, Jesus explained what became of the two of them after they died. (Incidentally, Lazarus is the only character given a name in any of Jesus' parables.) After a lifetime of indifference, the wealthy man was transported to hell. Here he at last became alive to the fate of the other man, who had been carried to *Abraham's bosom* by angels. Jews used this phrase to indicate the resting place of dead people favoured by God. It was a paradise of bliss and security. The expression carries with it a sense of privilege and honour – mirroring the way in which a father or master would allow a favoured servant or child to lean upon and gain security from his chest. Peter has

3

become recognised as the guardian of heaven for Christians, as the keeper of its keys and hence the lead character in many 'Pearly Gates' jokes, but the role of welcoming people to eternal glory for the Jews of Jesus' time belonged to the great father of faith, Abraham.

## Addicted

*I beseech you, brethren, (ye know the house of Stephanas, that it is the firstfruits of Achaia, and that they have addicted themselves to the ministry of the saints)*

1 Corinthians 16:15

If our children were to tell us that they were *addicted* we would be very worried, doubtless berating ourselves for having failed them in some way. In today's climate, any sort of addiction is considered a bad thing, as the object of the addiction is expected to be something harmful, like drugs. In the sixteenth century, though, the word *addicted* was invariably used to allude to positive qualities or values. So in 1 Corinthians 16:15 the apostle Paul writes of the addiction of certain Christians to ministering to others of the faith. Some translations express the phrase in terms of devotion, and state that they have devoted themselves to Christian service.

## Advertise

*And now, behold, I go unto my people: come therefore, and I will advertise thee what this people shall do to thy people in the latter days.*

**Numbers 24:14**

We live in a world that is saturated by advertising. Whether waiting at a bus stop, watching a programme on the television, listening to the radio or browsing through a magazine, we are continually bombarded with images and ideas that encourage us to buy a particular product or service. Our understanding of the word *advertise* is very different from its use in the Bible. There were none of our current commercial connotations then. The word meant to 'advise', 'warn' or even simply to 'tell' or 'let know'. In the verse quoted from Numbers the meaning is 'I will make clear to you what this people shall do to your people in the last days.'

## Affinity

*And Solomon made affinity with Pharaoh king of Egypt, and took Pharaoh's daughter, and brought her into the city of David, until he had made an end of building his own house, and the house of the Lord, and the wall of Jerusalem round about.*

**1 Kings 3:1**

From the passage quoted, it is clear that the word *affinity* carries the sense of making a treaty, pact or alliance. In times past, kingdoms have often sought to ease relations between themselves through marriage, and the rulers of biblical times were no exception to this custom. The strict use of the word referred to a relationship established through marriage. This differs from its use today, when *affinity* is used to describe a situation where a resemblance or special bond exists, and would be less likely to be used in a formal context.

## Alarm

Numbers 10:1–10

In modern experience an *alarm* is a disturbing device that destroys peaceful slumber and reminds us of the tyranny of work. Or when we get to work it is the device that is tested every Tuesday between 2 p.m. and 3 p.m. to keep Health and Safety happy. No wonder the word is also used to describe a sense of foreboding. The word actually comes from the Italian *all' arme*, 'to arms', and it is in this sense that it is used in Numbers 10:1–10, where it was used as a call to prepare for battle.

## All the days of my life

*Surely goodness and mercy shall follow me all the days of my life: and I will dwell in the house of the LORD for ever.*

**Psalm 23:6**

This expression breathes out the warmth and very essence of the much-loved Psalm 23 from which the expression derives. This timeless poem is treasured for its portrayal of the intimate friendship between the shepherd-king David and his God: a relationship of love, care and, above all, security and trust. The great king of Israel understood that his Shepherd provided help and support, not in a vague way across his life as a whole but in the specifics of each and every day: *all the days of his life*.

## All things to all men

*To the weak became I as weak, that I might gain the weak: I am made all things to all men, that I might by all means save some.*

**1 Corinthians 9:22**

The apostle Paul wasn't being sexist here – the original literally meant 'all things to all'. He was simply explaining his adaptable approach to the work of passing on his message. If someone expected him to be weak, he could

7

adapt his approach to seem as feeble as the next person. If they wanted an eighteen-stone body-builder he could do that too. Not literally, of course — rugged though he must have needed to be, it's unlikely that he would have pumped too much iron in the gym. He just wanted as many people as possible to think as he did, and if there was anything in his approach or manner that could present the slightest risk of putting up a barrier then he would change to make those around him feel more at home.

## The alpha and the omega

*I am Alpha and Omega, the beginning and the ending, saith the Lord, which is, and which was, and which is to come, the Almighty.*

Revelation 1:8

The *alpha* male in a pack of wolves may be quite literally the top dog and *omega* 3 oil may be the latest route to a healthy heart, but students of Greek know these two words respectively as the first and last letters of the Greek alphabet, so it's a bit like describing something as 'the A to Z of...' — in this case, of almighty God-ness. In Revelation 1:8 the expression comes from the lips of the Lord himself who describes himself as the One who is the present, the past and the future. He is not merely spread out at the bookends of history. Of course he was there at the beginning and he'll still be around at the end, but, equally importantly, he is the eternal *present*: the constant I AM, revealed first in his meeting with Moses and later through his incarnation in Jesus Christ.

## The apple of your eye

*He found him in a desert land, and in the waste howling wilderness; he led him about, he instructed him, he kept him as the apple of his eye.*

**Deuteronomy 32:10**

No modern physiology book would put it like this, but in the past the pupil of the eye was referred to as 'the apple'. After all, it is shaped roughly like one. In addition, because it is the most important part of the eye, *the apple of your eye* became a symbol of all things that were precious: the most valuable part of a highly valued part of the body. Dotted around the Bible the phrase therefore represents anything that is of great worth – whether it is the law of God in Proverbs 7:2, the people of Israel found and nurtured in the desert (Deuteronomy 32:10), or any individual on the receiving end of divine care.

# Armageddon

*And he gathered them together into a place called in the Hebrew tongue Armageddon.*

Revelation 16:16

The politics of the Cold War and the potential unleashing of catastrophic weapons upon the world led many doom-mongers to envisage that the earth was on the verge of *Armageddon*. This spine-chilling word is found in Revelation 16:16 and is the site, possibly originally meant for the mountain of Megiddo, where the last great battle between good and evil is to be fought. This awful day, the climax of God's intervention in history, is an occasion of unparalleled destruction, which explains why the phrase has come to be used as the archetypal expression of all that is dreadful for the human race. Hence the corny joke — 'I don't know what "Armageddon" means.' Response: 'Don't worry, it's not the end of the world.'

# Armhole

*And Ebed-melech the Ethiopian said unto Jeremiah, Put now these old cast clouts and rotten rags under thine armholes under the cords. And Jeremiah did so.*

Jeremiah 38:12

The poor prophet Jeremiah had been thrown into an unpleasant dungeon and left to rot. Fortunately for him, Ebed-melech knew of his whereabouts and went with some men to rescue him. In order to pull him out of the ground, they threw down a rope. His rescuer then threw down some rags so that Jeremiah could place the ropes under his arms using the rags for padding. He was then hauled to safety. It is clear from this episode that *armholes* are not the openings in an item of clothing which we might put our hands through. Instead, the word meant what we would refer to today as our armpits.

# B

## Balthazar

*See* **Jeroboam**

## Barbarian

*I am debtor both to the Greeks, and to the Barbarians;*
*both to the wise, and to the unwise.*

**Romans 1:14**

Today if we call someone a *barbarian* we usually mean that they are uncouth and badly behaved. In the past, the term meant more simply (and less judgementally) 'foreigner'. It was originally applied by Greeks to the non-Greek-speaking world, gradually changing its meaning to apply to all those who were rude and lacking in good breeding and civilisation. Other nations took up the concept of defining themselves as the quality nation and dismissing others as barbarians. Thus, after the Greeks, the Romans came to apply it to all non-Romans; in 2 Maccabees in the Apocrypha it is used by

13

the Jews of the Gentiles and even if the word of the moment changes, the concept of comparing others unfavourably to ourselves will doubtless continue into the foreseeable future. Here though, Paul shows the even-handedness more fully developed elsewhere: all can make a contribution to God's kingdom.

## The beam in your eye

*Thou hypocrite, first cast out the beam out of thine own eye; and then shalt thou see clearly to cast out the mote out of thy brother's eye.*

Matthew 7:5

Anyone who has had to drive at night towards an oncoming car that has not dipped its headlights will know something of the discomfort of having a beam in the eye. The beam in question here, however, is a large piece of wood. Jesus, in a section of the Sermon on the Mount recorded by Matthew, was speaking against hypocrites who, while peering into someone else's eye in order to extract a speck of dust, fail to realise that their own vision is itself obscured by an absurdly huge block of timber. He is commenting upon our remarkable ability to spot the faults and failings of others, despite being oblivious to our own. When we tell someone to take *the beam out of their own eye*, we are simply asking them to sort themselves out first and then, should they still wish to be critical, they may make some claim to sort out someone else's vision. Best to check first, though, as to the clarity of your own vision.

## Bear the burden and heat of the day

*These last have wrought but one hour, and thou hast made them equal unto us, which have borne the burden and heat of the day.*

**Matthew 20:12**

The phrase *the burden and heat of the day* emphasises the hard nature of manual work outdoors. Its origins lie in the story Jesus told of the vineyard owner who wanted to hire workers. He hired workers in stages from early morning onwards and throughout the day. When, at the end of the day, the boss decided to pay all his workers the same wage, irrespective of how long they had worked, those who had slogged it out since the beginning of the day were, unsurprisingly, somewhat upset. They voiced their concern over the blatant injustice of it all — after all, they had been taken on when it was early morning, yet only received the same wage as those who had been taken on almost at the end of the working

15

day. Their complaint fell on deaf ears. The challenge is to be grateful when we are given as much or more than our due, even if others seem to be even more generously treated.

## Beating swords into ploughshares

*And he shall judge among the nations, and shall rebuke many people: and they shall beat their swords into plowshares, and their spears into pruninghooks: nation shall not lift up sword against nation, neither shall they learn war any more.*

Isaiah 2:4

This powerful expression occurs in Isaiah 2:4 and Micah 4:3. These verses refer to a future time when there will be no more need for the instruments of warfare. And rather than being left to rust in a gigantic stockpile to be picked up again next time there's a disagreement, there will be such confidence in their redundancy that they are decommissioned for good through their transformation into farming implements. Weapons are converted into tools to cultivate the soil. The phrase carries with it a sense of finality, reinforced by the context in the Bible when a golden age is ushered in by God himself. That will be an age of peace, an age where there is neither the need nor any inclination to take up arms.

## The blind leading the blind

*Let them alone: they be blind leaders of the blind. And if the blind lead the blind, both shall fall into the ditch.*

**Matthew 15:14**

Nothing could be more ridiculous than the idea of one sightless individual taking another by the hand and attempting to guide him along a twisting path or busy street. It is this absurd situation that Jesus used in Matthew 15:14 to describe the Pharisees. The inference was both funny and humiliating: they didn't know what they were talking about, but nevertheless insisted upon passing on their lack of understanding to others. No one wants to be led by someone who can't see properly – especially when their own vision is impaired. Although the original meaning attacks the arrogance of those who ought to be qualified to guide others but aren't, the phrase is now commonly used more loosely, to describe what happens when a novice in any area attempts to guide another newcomer: *You've only been working here for two weeks and you're trying to lead the induction course. If that's not the blind leading the blind, I don't know what is!*

## Bone of my bones

*And Adam said, This is now bone of my bones, and flesh of my flesh: she shall be called Woman, because she was taken out of Man.*

**Genesis 2:23**

In the first chapters of the Bible, God creates a companion for the first man, Adam. To do this he uses a rib, plucked from Adam's body itself. When he has completed his task and presents the new creation to Adam, the appreciative man proclaims his unabashed delight. Obscured by translation, in the original Hebrew Adam's shout of pleasure carries with it the idea of unrivalled excellence – the best of the best. There has been a tendency to see woman as subordinate since she was taken out of man, but the grateful recipient of this gift of a companion saw it as an incomparable present, excelling even himself: in every way the best a man can get.

## Born again

*Jesus answered and said unto him, Verily, verily, I say unto thee, Except a man be born again, he cannot see the kingdom of God.*

**John 3:3**

In many circles today the caricature of a 'born-again' Christian is that of an earnest individual, too zealous for his or her own good. Too keen. Too 'in your face'. And not very British. The words belong to Jesus in a conversation of which this verse is the lynchpin. They seemed to shock the person he was talking to as much as they offend people today. Jesus said that to see God's kingdom, his friend had to be born again. What has become something of a cliché was here a startling expression encapsulating the idea of a radical rebirth, a new beginning as completely different from what went before as breathing air is different from the containment of the womb. A wholesale spiritual re-awakening.

## Botch

*The Lord will smite thee with the botch of Egypt, and with the emerods, and with the scab, and with the itch, whereof thou canst not be healed.*

**Deuteronomy 28:27**

If you were to ask my wife for a definition of the word *botch*, it could well contain the words 'husband', 'DIY' and 'job'. And rightly so. In this verse from Deuteronomy, which describes a curse Moses threatens against the Israelites should they forsake God, the word *botch* refers to a boil or sores. Elsewhere in the King James Version, the same Hebrew word is rendered as *boil* or *boils*. The distinct translation of the word gave rise to the notion that it referred to a particularly unpleasant disease, but this is not the case. And it is has clearly gone through successive meaning changes to arrive at the word we use today.

## Bowels

*Put on therefore, as the elect of God, holy and beloved, bowels of mercies, kindness, humbleness of mind, meekness, longsuffering.*

**Colossians 3:12**

We are quite used to seeing car stickers announcing 'I ❤ NY' or 'I ❤ my dog.' We might not be so comfortable if the heart were replaced by a representation of bowels. Yet to the writers of the King James Version, the heart and the *bowels* were both regarded as the home for emotions. So in a list of qualities Paul expects Christians to show, he includes 'bowels of mercies' to describe a compassionate, caring nature. Perhaps, though, this is just not an image we want to think about too closely.

## Bravery

*In that day the Lord will take away the bravery of their
tinkling ornaments about their feet, and their cauls, and
their round tires like the moon.*

Isaiah 3:18

*Bravery* is a quality that we display in the face of great peril
or danger. It seems an unusual word to use of women's
jewellery. This is because it actually referred to their
finery – what we might call 'glad rags' today. Isaiah was
warning the rich, arrogant Jewish women, who spent
too much time pandering to their own looks and appear-
ances, that if they continued in this way, one day all that
outward beauty would be taken away, revealing nothing
but their spiritual ugliness. What is interesting is the link
between these two sorts of bravery: both have clear
external expression as a major element.

## Burden

*The burden of Nineveh. The book of the vision of Nahum
the Elkoshite.*

Nahum 1:1

In today's English, a *burden* is a large, heavy object that
is difficult to carry, or some onerous situation that weighs

down the heart and soul of a person. The King James Version uses this same sense, but it has another slant too. It can also mean 'oracle', so Nahum's book is about an oracle, or message concerning the city of Nineveh. The word burden is also used in this sense by other prophets including Isaiah, Jeremiah and Zechariah; perhaps not unfittingly considering the personal hardship they went through in their prophetic careers and the harsh words they often had to deliver to the Jewish people.

# C

*༻•༺*

## A camel going through the eye of a needle

*And again I say unto you, It is easier for a camel to go through the eye of a needle, than for a rich man to enter into the kingdom of God.*

Matthew 19:24

Imagine your average zoo keeper getting into a conversation with an expert in embroidery – surely both would agree that if it should cross anyone's mind to take a camel and squeeze it through the tiny hole on a sewing implement, the chances of success would be slim, if not non-existent. Camels are big, needle eyes are not, and therefore, with the best will in the world, it cannot be done. Jesus, when he came up with this vivid phrase, knew that was the case. That's why it suited his purpose so well. He wanted an illustration of the impossible, because he was trying to explain to his followers that there was no way a rich man could get into God's kingdom by his own efforts. We're sure camels, embroiderers, zoo keepers and disciples all get the point.

# Cast the first stone

*So when they continued asking him, he lifted up himself, and said unto them, He that is without sin among you, let him first cast a stone at her.*

John 8:7

*Let him cast the first stone* is how this phrase is some-times expressed, although the King James Version actually says 'first cast a stone'. A woman who had been caught committing adultery was brought to Jesus. Her accusers expected Jesus to bring down on her the full force of the Mosaic law: execution by stoning. Instead of judging her, however, he invited individuals of the lynch party to apply the law themselves by beginning the execution – but only if they were sinless. Only those who have never disobeyed the law are truly in a posi-tion to administer its exacting demands. So today the phrase is used as a sobering wake-up call to anyone who is quick to demand harsh justice for others, to make them think again as to their own qualifications as a judge.

# Castaway

*I therefore so run, not as uncertainly; so fight I, not as one that beateth the air: but I keep under my body, and bring*

*it into subjection: lest that by any means, when I have*
*preached to others, I myself should be a castaway.*

1 Corinthians 9:26–27

The word *castaway* conjures up visions of Tom Hanks stuck on a remote island in the middle of the Pacific, or the more literary reference of Robinson Crusoe sharing a similar fate. It conjures up for us a slightly romantic vision of desert sands, palm trees and some poor traveller struggling to reach the shore after a shipwreck, only to discover that in addition to finding the works of Shakespeare and the Bible, he or she is also allowed to listen to their eight favourite pieces of music. In the past, however, it meant someone who was not suitable for a task, particularly an unfit athlete. This is the way Paul uses it in his first letter to the Corinthians as he outlines his concern to do everything he possibly can so that, at the end of his ministry, he will not be excluded from the benefits he has been extolling to others.

## Casting pearls before swine

*Give not that which is holy unto the dogs, neither cast ye*
*your pearls before swine, lest they trample them under*
*their feet, and turn again and rend you.*

Matthew 7:6

In the days of Jesus, even more so than today, pearls were immensely valuable objects that everyone could admire and appreciate. And while we might consider cooked bacon for breakfast a treat, pigs were (and still are) 'unclean' animals for Jews. So on both counts this illustration was even more powerful for its initial audience than it is for us – but even for us it's clear that creatures that appear unable to see beyond the next mouthful wouldn't know what to do with an expensive pearl necklace that really ought to adorn the graceful neck of a beautiful woman. If they didn't gobble them along with their revolting offal, they would certainly cover them in mud and worse, so robbing the pearls of their beauty and dignity. The lesson is: do not waste valuable things on those who are incapable of appreciating them – do not *cast pearls before swine*.

## Chambering

*Let us walk honestly, as in the day; not in rioting and drunkenness, not in chambering and wantonness, not in strife and envying.*

**Romans 13:13**

*Chambering*, a word that has become obsolete since it was first used here in Tyndale's translation, means 'sexual excesses'. It appears in a list of activities to be avoided in Paul's letter to the Romans. Current versions translate the same word in phrases such as *sexual licence*, *debauchery*, *promiscuity* or *immorality*. The quaint use of 'chamber' euphemistically suggests the primary location where such behaviour is expected to take place. This makes quite a contrast with the romantic and fairy-tale connotations which the word 'chamber' is more likely to have for today's reader, as in 'my lady's chamber'.

## Chargeable

*And the king said to Absalom, Nay, my son, let us not all now go, lest we be chargeable unto thee. And he pressed him: howbeit he would not go, but blessed him.*

2 Samuel 13:25

Though its fundamental meaning has not changed, often today *chargeable* ends up with a positive meaning – we might read that the first two tickets for something may be purchased for £20 each, but the next one is not chargeable. Or an expense turns out to be chargeable against tax. In the King James Version the same word is used in a wider sense of being a burden or nuisance to someone, not just financially. So in 2 Samuel 13:25 King David didn't want to go to join his son Absalom at the time of sheep shearing becuase he did not want to be a burden to him.

## Charity

*And now abideth faith, hope, charity, these three; but the greatest of these is charity.*

**1 Corinthians 13:13**

*Charity* makes many of us today think of people harassing us in the streets for a 'moment of your time', or of endless phone-ins on the television. It is something we give to in order to help others. We are rightly encouraged to be kind and generous to those who are less well off than ourselves. The word is used in 1 Corinthians 13 when Paul talks about the supremacy of love, and therefore should surely carry a greater call to give to others out of love, not just duty. This chapter is often asked for by couples at their marriage service. The original Greek word is translated as *love* on 86 occasions and as *charity* 26 times in the King James Version. It is difficult to understand fully why this should be the case. Its use in the Corinthians passage may be due to the fact that even by the time the King James Version was written the passage had become well known and memorised, and therefore there was some reluctance to change such a familiar passage.

# The chosen few

*For many are called, but few are chosen.*

**Matthew 22:14**

If a person belongs to the chosen few, he or she is in the privileged position of being in a group that, for whatever reason, is deemed to be especially fortunate. The origins of this expression lie in Jesus' story about a wedding. The groom happened to be the king's son. The king invited countless people to attend the event, but in reply to every invitation came an excuse for not attending. So the king ordered that the highways and byways be scoured for people to share in his family's happiness. Yet even in his eagerness to have as many as possible share in his son's special day, the king retained regal standards. As he strolled about during the festivities, he came across a guest who wasn't wearing the appropriate wedding garments and called for him to be expelled from the wedding festivities.

# The chosen people

*But ye are a chosen generation, a royal priesthood, an holy nation, a peculiar people; that ye should shew forth the praises of him who hath called you out of darkness into his marvellous light.*

**1 Peter 2:9**

The *chosen people* is a phrase that has been used by different religious groups throughout history to describe how they feel about themselves and their beliefs. In the Old Testament the Jews are God's chosen people. They had been selected by God in order to be the object of his special care and love, as well as being his representatives on earth. This perspective changes in the New Testament. When Jesus Christ first appears in the pages of the Gospels, the Jews see themselves at the centre of God's world. Jesus himself gave hints of a broadening of the scope of God's choice. By the time Peter wrote of a chosen generation, the chosen ones were understood to be all those who believed in the message of Jesus Christ. The phrase has since been understood to have particular meaning for them by different peoples through history.

## A chosen vessel

*But the Lord said unto him, Go thy way: for he is a chosen vessel unto me, to bear my name before the Gentiles, and kings, and the children of Israel.*

**Acts 9:15**

A vessel in today's language is an object associated with transport. The object could be something that helps blood course around the body, a boat navigating the oceans or a container full of liquid. The phrase *chosen vessel* relates to a person who has been given a special task to perform. To continue the analogy, he or she acts as a channel along which an action or message can flow. Like other vessels they have been commissioned to perform a task. In the New Testament, Paul was selected by God to be such a vessel. His task was to take God's name and message not just to his Jewish compatriots, but also to Gentiles (or non-Jews), to rich and poor alike.

## Clothed and in your right mind

*Then they went out to see what was done; and came to Jesus, and found the man, out of whom the devils were departed, sitting at the feet of Jesus, clothed, and in his right mind: and they were afraid.*

Luke 8:35

Someone who is *clothed and in their right mind* has their faculties, abilities and manner fully in order and ready to face a specific activity. Usually there is a suggestion of contrast between that state and a real or hypothetical one of chaos and unpreparedness. You might therefore use the phrase to reassure someone else that, contrary to their expectations, all is well – 'You may think I'm mad, but I'm actually all right.' In the story from which the phrase originates, a man who had previously been tormented and driven to despair, destruction and rampant nudity by evil spirits was now, in striking contrast, behaving in a completely normal manner. He was even wearing clothes again!

## A cloud no bigger than a man's hand

*And it came to pass at the seventh time, that he said, Behold, there ariseth a little cloud out of the sea, like a man's hand. And he said, Go up, say unto Ahab, Prepare thy chariot, and get thee down, that the rain stop thee not.*

1 Kings 18:44

The point here is that what begins as a small cloud at a great distance quickly demands to be viewed in a different light as it develops into a dark storm cloud, heavy with rain and being blown in their direction! Elijah, fresh from his success as God's agent against the false prophets of Baal, prayed for relief from the drought that had been afflicting Israel. He went with his servant to see what would happen. At first there was no sign at all, but eventually Elijah's servant noticed a cloud – the first, scarcely visible, proof that God's answer was on its way. Something small and barely noticed may become significant with surprising speed – so be aware!

## Comfortless

*I will not leave you comfortless: I will come to you.*

John 14:18

*Comfortless*, an archaic word meaning 'destitute', is seldom heard in modern English. In Greek the word used is *orphanos*, from which the word *orphan* comes. It is this word that is often used in contemporary versions and though it has a specific technical meaning for us, it nonetheless fits well with Jesus' words, as he promised his disciples that he would not leave them on their own, but, would still be with them through his Spirit, even when physically he was no longer present.

## Consider the lilies

*And why take ye thought for raiment? Consider the lilies of the field, how they grow; they toil not, neither do they spin: And yet I say unto you, That even Solomon in all his glory was not arrayed like one of these.*

Matthew 6:28–29

Anyone who has been to Monet's house at Giverny will be able to understand the driving force behind this command. His famous Impressionist paintings of the water lilies were painted there, and the beauty of these lilies is impossible to ignore. When Jesus challenged his listeners to reflect upon lilies he was urging them to move away from their own concerns and worries about material goods and needs. Lilies (probably not actually water lilies here, but the image holds) are amazing – their colours, shapes and beauty far exceeding anything that the great King Solomon could come up with. Yet, for all that, they never actually did anything. They didn't have to, because God provided everything that was necessary. The challenge to Jesus' followers is to trust him to look after their lives too.

## Consult

*Thou hast consulted shame to thy house by cutting off many people, and hast sinned against thy soul.*

**Habakkuk 2:10**

When we want a viewpoint on a matter upon which we have little or no expertise we go and consult an expert or use a reference book, dictionary or some similar means in order to get the knowledge or wisdom we need.

In the King James Version the word is used in this sense, but it also has another meaning. In Habakkuk it carries the idea of planning or devising. So the passage might equally be rendered 'You have deliberately brought shame to your house.'

## Conversation

*That ye put off concerning the former conversation the old man, which is corrupt according to the deceitful lusts;*

**Ephesians 4:22**

A *conversation*, in the twenty-first century, is a discussion, dialogue or other form of talk between two or more individuals. It is specifically a verbal interaction. In the King James Version the word *conversation* has a different meaning, however. It stands for a person's behaviour, conduct or way of life. In the above verse from Ephesians, Paul is urging his readers to change the way they behave; he therefore tells them to leave behind the 'former conversation' – their old habits and ways.

# Count the cost

*For which of you, intending to build a tower, sitteth not down first, and counteth the cost, whether he have sufficient to finish it?*

Luke 14:28

Each of us at one time or another has been challenged to consider the consequences of our actions, whether as a toddler daring to confront his or her parents, a teenager about to embark on some undesirable activities, or newlyweds wondering if they can afford the mortgage on their dream home. Before rushing into something that seems exciting, perfect, necessary – take time to reflect. As it says on the adverts for investment products, 'Share prices can go down as well as up'. What seems like a good idea may indeed turn out to be so, but are you sure that you've considered carefully enough? This is what the sensible person will do, whether or not the main risk is financial. Sit down, take stock, write out the pros and cons to see if that dream can become a reality: that is counting the cost.

# Cover a multitude of sins

*And above all things have fervent charity among*
*yourselves: for charity shall cover the multitude of sins.*

1 Peter 4:8

It is shockingly easy to harbour grudges and allow resentment to take root, blossom and flourish – especially where we feel that we have been harshly treated by another person. When we believe ourselves to be the victim of some wrong or injustice, our resentment – not to mention our ability to quantify and classify each wound – builds. Peter's remedy for this festering cancer that can destroy both individuals and groups is love. As the King James Version puts it, *charity shall cover the multitude of sins*. It neither ignores them nor pretends they don't exist. It knows they are real and it takes them seriously, but nevertheless chooses to cover them so they needn't be brought out into the open for all to see. Often the expression is heard in situations where something good is held to make up for whatever faults and mistakes there are and the latter are deliberately overlooked.

## Cover your feet

*When he was gone out, his servants came; and when they saw that, behold, the doors of the parlour were locked, they said, Surely he covereth his feet in his summer chamber.*

Judges 3:24

We have never been comfortable with describing bodily functions. Rather than saying 'He's urinating' we might remark that 'He's spending a penny'. The euphemisms are endless. In the King James Version this same desire to obfuscate such activities is present. The story related in Judges 3 concerns a man, King Eglon, who had been killed and left by his assailant, the judge Ehud. The servants were concerned by their master's non-appearance, but also worried about going in to see if he was all right in case he was sitting on the toilet, *covering his feet*. The expression comes from the fact that during this period of squatting, the person's robes and garments would cover their feet. Fortunately this is one phrase where its usage today is entirely straightforward.

# Crumbs from the rich man's table

*And she said, Truth, Lord: yet the dogs eat of the crumbs which fall from their masters' table.*

**Matthew 15:27**

*And there was a certain beggar named Lazarus, which was laid at his gate, full of sores, and desiring to be fed with the crumbs which fell from the rich man's table: moreover the dogs came and licked his sores.*

**Luke 16:20–21**

One of the useful aspects of owning a dog is that it cuts down on the cleaning-up of those inevitable accidents that occur in the kitchen. A quick, 'Here, boy!' and the obedient hound pads over and hoovers up the mess. They will vacuum up the unnoticed bits of food too. So when someone talks about crumbs that fall from the table, their observation is based on the practicalities of domestic life – as in Palestine all those years ago, so today. When the rich of this world have finished with anything, the poor have their opportunity to benefit from the leftovers – whether that is food, possessions or wealth. The use of the saying in the New Testament is all the more poignant because dogs were not given the same affection they receive in our pet-loving society. They were opportunistic scavengers that lived as outcasts on the margins of society – not a good position in which to find oneself.

## My cup runs over

*Thou preparest a table before me in the presence of mine enemies: thou anointest my head with oil; my cup runneth over.*

**Psalm 23:5**

Anyone who has children will understand the practical implications of the expression *my cup runneth over*: cloths or kitchen roll will be required urgently. When someone talks of their cup running over, what they mean is that they are experiencing more than enough of something. It's almost as if they are brimming over. The concept still usually refers to something that is enjoyable or valuable, though it may be used sarcastically as well.

## The curse/mark of Cain

*And he said, What hast thou done? the voice of thy brother's blood crieth unto me from the ground. And now art thou cursed from the earth, which hath opened her mouth to receive thy brother's blood from thy hand; when thou tillest the ground, it shall not henceforth yield unto thee her strength; a fugitive and a vagabond shalt thou be in the earth.*

**Genesis 4:10–12**

The *curse of Cain* and the *mark of Cain* are actually two slightly different expressions. The former describes the fate of an outlaw, perpetually fleeing from one location to the next like a fugitive on the run from the law. The latter is invoked when someone's character is stained, usually through a crime or some act of notoriety. Both stem from the same early part of the Bible where God curses Cain for having killed his brother. Having done that, he immediately guarantees his future safety by placing upon him the equivalent of a 'Do not touch' sign to all potential murderers. It is intriguing how the sense of the *mark of Cain* has changed, losing the idea of God's protection and mercy, leaving only the sense of stigma. Perhaps it shows that human thought patterns are less gracious and forgiving than God's.

# D

◦─────◦

## Our daily bread

*Give us this day our daily bread.*

Matthew 6:11

*Daily bread* is the food you need in order to continue to live. More broadly, it can refer to the wider physical necessities of life, such as clothing, housing and the resources to secure these items. In some cultures, rice or another staple occupies the same level of importance, so there is nothing implicitly special about 'bread' — the point, rather, is what it represents. In Jewish culture, it was the basic requirement for any meal. But it was also critical to some of the most important feasts in the religious calendar, such as unleavened bread for Passover. In addition, its association with the manna that was miraculously given to the Israelites as they wandered through the desert guaranteed that the thoughtful person would notice the divine link between the provision of physical and spiritual requirements.

# A Damascus-road experience

*And as he journeyed, he came near Damascus: and suddenly there shined round about him a light from heaven: and he fell to the earth, and heard a voice saying unto him, Saul, Saul, why persecutest thou me? And he said, Who art thou, Lord? And the Lord said, I am Jesus whom thou persecutest: it is hard for thee to kick against the pricks. And he trembling and astonished said, Lord, what wilt thou have me to do? And the Lord said unto him, Arise, and go into the city, and it shall be told thee what thou must do.*

Acts 9:3–6

If someone has a *road to Damascus experience*, he or she undergoes a radical experience which deeply changes their point of view – possibly, as here, conversion to a radically different set of beliefs. Similarly, they might say that they have *seen the light*. Both these expressions have their origins in the accounts in the Acts of the Apostles of the conversion of Saul of Tarsus. He had been travelling to Damascus set on causing as much trouble as possible to the embryonic church. As he journeyed he was suddenly overcome by a bright light from heaven. This led to him abandoning his Jewish faith and embracing the new religion based upon the teachings of Jesus of Nazareth. Nowadays the expression is often parodied, most notably in the film *The Blues Brothers* when

Jake had an epiphany in which a bright spotlight shone down from heaven while he was attending a church service.

# David and Goliath

1 Samuel 17

A *David and Goliath* situation is one in which two rivals come face to face and the less fancied succeeds in getting the better of the favourite. It is used a great deal in sport to describe an upset where perhaps a lesser team or individual 'underdog' manages to score a notable victory over a well-known, better prepared one. The original David was a shepherd boy, the youngest of eight brothers who served in the Israelite army. Goliath was a giant of a man, a Philistine and professional soldier, heavily clad in protective armour. The two met in a 'winner-takes-all' scenario and against all the odds, David – who was only lightly armed, with a slingshot – managed to unleash a stone that found a chink in his opponent's protection. Goliath crashed to the ground and the triumphant David, much to the horror of the Philistine ranks, proceeded to decapitate the stricken warrior.

# Day of small things

*See* **Do not despise the day of small things**

# Debate

*Being filled with all unrighteousness, fornication, wickedness, covetousness, maliciousness; full of envy, murder, debate, deceit, malignity; whisperers.*

**Romans 1:29**

Even if we have watched our elected representatives lock horns in the House of Commons, it is unlikely that any of us would categorise their behaviour with such a range of evils as Paul does in Romans 1. In this chapter he lists a variety of sins that characterise godlessness, and *debate* finds itself sandwiched between murder and deceit. What it means in this context is 'strife'. This old use is therefore not unrelated to the kind of debate one might find at the Oxford Union, but is at the extreme end: debate with a clear intention to cause dissension, rather than to achieve an ultimately united resolution. It is for this reason that it takes its place in a list of no-go areas for Christians.

# Delicacy

*For all nations have drunk of the wine of the wrath of her fornication, and the kings of the earth have committed fornication with her, and the merchants of the earth are waxed rich through the abundance of her delicacies.*

**Revelation 18:3**

Those of us who enjoy our food look forward with special delight to tasting some well-prepared delicacy, such as might be enjoyed at a special festive occasion. In the King James Version the word was used to describe a pleasurable experience, but of a totally different type. Here the word has sexual connotations and expresses the idea of an erotic or sensual indulgence. The passage in Revelation describes the city of Babylon, the archetypal location of all that is wicked, and portrays it as a place of every kind of indulgence including the gratification of sexual lusts and improper desire.

# Delilah

**Judges 16:4–31**

If a woman is a described as a *Delilah*, it means that, precisely because she is so alluring, she is unlikely to be someone to be trusted. The original Delilah was

47

certainly such a woman. Samson fell in love with her and, when his enemies heard of their relationship, they bribed her into obtaining the secret of his phenomenal strength. Initially, he kept his secret close to his chest. Delilah tried to prise the information from him on three occasions, but perhaps because he was wary of her motives (after the first time, when he woke to find Philistine soldiers trying to ensnare him, how could he not be?), he lied to her each time. Finally, after her continual nagging, he gave in and explained that his strength lay in his uncut hair. Later, when he fell asleep in her company, she betrayed him to the Philistines, who promptly shaved his head, depriving him of his God-given power. At this point, the Philistines – confident their enemy was significantly weakened – appeared and captured him. Samson was blinded and held captive by his enemies, but he finally had the last laugh when he single-handedly destroyed their temple and all those inside.

## A den of thieves

*And Jesus went into the temple of God, and cast out all them that sold and bought in the temple, and overthrew the tables of the moneychangers, and the seats of them that sold doves, and said unto them, It is written, My*

*house shall be called the house of prayer; but ye have made
it a den of thieves.*

Matthew 21:12–13

A *den of thieves* is a place where crooks and robbers hang
out. The word *den*, which is often used to describe the
home of wild animals, conjures up the idea of a secretive place intended for exclusive use by the owners, not
what you would expect of the Temple, God's dwelling
place on earth. When Jesus used this expression, alluding
to an earlier use in Jeremiah, he brought with it the full
force of divine condemnation against those who had
turned the holy Temple of God, with the presence of
divinity, into a squalid lair for disreputable characters
and equally dodgy practices.

## Divide the sheep from the goats

*And before him shall be gathered all nations: and he shall
separate them one from another, as a shepherd divideth
his sheep from the goats: and he shall set the sheep on his
right hand, but the goats on the left.*

Matthew 25:32–33

If you *divide* or *separate the sheep from the goats*, you sort
people or things into two groups: the useful and the
useless. Jesus used this farming imagery to describe the

49

way in which eternal judgement would be carried out. The sheep were to receive the Father's blessing of eternal life while the goats would be banished into eternal punishment. The use of the analogy is particularly poignant in a Middle Eastern setting because, compared to Western farm animals, sheep and goats in Israel were, and still are, far harder to distinguish. Jesus was therefore making a harder-hitting point than may be immediately apparent to us today: the similarity in many ways of the two groups highlights the skill of the shepherd in making the correct choice about where to place each particular animal.

## Do as you would be done by

*See* The **golden rule**

## Do not despise the day of small things

*For who hath despised the day of small things? for they shall rejoice, and shall see the plummet in the hand of Zerubbabel with those seven; they are the eyes of the Lord, which run to and fro through the whole earth.*

Zechariah 4:10

It's very easy to look down on people or events that appear to be insignificant or have minimal importance. In a world that clamours for the brash, the loud and the latest self-aggrandising trumpet blower, the quiet, the humble and the good things which apparently insignificant people bring about are easily overlooked, or if seen, are ridiculed and mocked. This saying takes the opposite view. The admonition of those who *despise the day of small things* is a clarion call against the seemingly insatiable thirst to slake the attention-seeking needs of the brash. The image of a 'plummet' (plumb-line) in the hands of a worker such as Zerubbabel as he laid the foundation in the rebuilding of the Temple is as deep as the stones themselves. Anyone looking at the completed majesty of God's house would do well to remember the humble beginnings from which the mighty structure began.

## Do to others as you would have them do to you

*See* The **golden rule**

## Doctor

*And it came to pass, that after three days they found him in the temple, sitting in the midst of the doctors, both hearing them, and asking them questions.*

**Luke 2:46**

The most common way in which we understand the word *doctor* today is when we are referring to someone who is qualified to treat the various illnesses and ailments that beset us. The original meaning of the word was 'teacher', which explains why those who have acquired specialist knowledge in a particular field may also earn the title doctor. In Luke 2:46, the young Jesus has stayed in Jerusalem, rather than returning home with his parents. They eventually found him in the Temple discussing spiritual matters with the religious leaders and teachers or doctors of the Jewish law.

## A doubting Thomas

*But Thomas, one of the twelve, called Didymus, was not with them when Jesus came. The other disciples therefore said unto him, We have seen the Lord. But he said unto them, Except I shall see in his hands the print of the nails, and put my finger into the print of the nails, and thrust my hand into his side, I will not believe.*

John 20:24–25

A *doubting Thomas* is anyone who demands concrete proof or evidence in order to believe. Such a person is incapable of relying upon the words of another person. They have to see, touch and hear with their own eyes, hands and ears. The original *doubting Thomas* was one of Jesus' disciples who had been absent when Jesus came back to life and appeared to some of his other followers. When they tried to explain to their absent friend what had happened, he resolutely refused to believe them. The only thing that would convince him, he told them, was if he himself could see and feel the wounds in Jesus' side and his hands. A week later, when Jesus himself again appeared to his friends, he invited Thomas to do the very things the reluctant disciple had claimed would allay his doubts. In fact it seems that when it came to it he did not need the hard physical proof he'd asked for: there and then he acknowledged Jesus as his Lord and his God.

## Draught

*For he was astonished, and all that were with him, at the draught of the fishes which they had taken.*

**Luke 5:9**

*And they brake down the image of Baal, and brake down the house of Baal, and made it a draught house unto this day.*

**2 Kings 10:27**

If we take a *draught* in the *draught*, we might well mean that we are consuming a quantity of liquid in one swallow, while at the same time experiencing a slight current of cold air. It is highly unlikely that we mean we have caught a load of fish in the toilet. Nevertheless this latter explanation could theoretically have been possible to readers of the King James Version. This is because the word *draught* had two possible meanings: 'a catch of fish' and 'toilet' or 'latrine'. In Luke 5:9 Jesus had asked Peter to throw his net back into the water after an unsuccessful night's fishing. When the disciples acted on Jesus' words they found, to their utter amazement, that the nets were teeming with fish when they tried to haul them in. In 2 Kings 10:27 an incident is described in which the temple of a false god, Baal, was demolished, and from the rubble a rough and ready public toilet emerged. Pious Jews may have used the facilities with great delight at the opportunity to show their distaste towards the building's original use!

## To draw a bow at a venture

*And a certain man drew a bow at a venture, and smote the king of Israel between the joints of the harness: wherefore he said unto the driver of his chariot, Turn thine hand, and carry me out of the host; for I am wounded.*

1 Kings 22:34

The word *venture* has several possible meanings today, most of which carry some sense of excitement, danger and enterprise. So an explorer may embark on a venture through the jungle. Similarly, it can be used when you want to express an opinion in a non-confrontational manner: 'I *venture* to suggest that you are wrong.' When in the King James Version we read the expression *at a venture* it means 'at random'. So in the verse from 1 Kings 22, an archer simply fired an arrow towards the opposing army without a particular aim, but it happened to strike the king by chance.

## A drop in the bucket/ocean

*Behold, the nations are as a drop of a bucket, and are counted as the small dust of the balance: behold, he taketh up the isles as a very little thing.*

Isaiah 40:15

A *drop in the bucket* is an insignificant quantity when compared with the contents of a bucket or the vastly larger ocean. So the idea being alluded to here is that of insignificance when set alongside something that is immeasurably greater. The verses could seem to imply that God shows contempt for the nations, but the real sense is that the nations are so small and insignificant compared with him that he is not intimidated by them in the slightest: he takes notice of them because he chooses to, not because they can force him to. The expression is frequently used to describe what happens when someone performs an apparently futile action that is perceived to have no impact upon a situation. In the context, Isaiah is explaining how from a divine perspective, even the mighty nations appear minute. They are rather like a speck of dust that has found its way onto a set of scales – unlikely to be seen and certainly failing to register any increase in weight. Or like the view of the world we get from a plane – tiny from our lofty perspective. God is incomparably greater than us.

# E

## Ear

*For these two years hath the famine been in the land: and
yet there are five years, in the which there shall neither be
earing nor harvest.*

Genesis 45:6

Everybody knows what an *ear* is. It is the organ of hearing,
or the word may be used to describe the part of a cereal
that contains the seed. In former times, however, the
word carried another idea. It could also mean 'to plough'
in the sense of making ground ready for planting. This
will explain the verse in Genesis 45:6 that does not refer
to a period without jewellery or harvest, but to a time
in which there would be no ploughing or planting and
consequently there wouldn't be a harvest.

## Eat, drink and be merry, for tomorrow we die

*And behold joy and gladness, slaying oxen, and killing*

*sheep, eating flesh, and drinking wine: let us eat and drink;
for tomorrow we shall die.*

Isaiah 22:13

When we say, *let's eat, drink and be merry* – with or without
its corollary, *for tomorrow we die*, the call is to enjoy ourselves
while we can, because we don't know what the future may
hold. It may come as a surprise to discover that this well-
known saying and its variations occur three times in the
Bible. It seems to be advocating a life of hedonistic enjoy-
ment: you may as well get what you can out of existence
because sooner or later it is going to come to an end. The
reality is that on two of these occurrences the viewpoint
elicits disapproval: in Isaiah the city of Jerusalem is being
condemned for its inappropriate behaviour, and when it
is cited in Jesus' parable in Luke 12 the words are uttered
by a man labelled as a rich fool. Only in Ecclesiastes 8 is
the phrase tempered by the acknowledgement, in the last
verse of the book, that God will ultimately judge everyone's
conduct. In reality therefore, the self-indulgent outlook
is not being encouraged, but condemned. It might be a valid
philosophy in a meaningless world, but it has no place in
the world the Bible describes.

# The eleventh hour

*And about the eleventh hour he went out, and found others standing idle, and saith unto them, Why stand ye here all the day idle?*

**Matthew 20:6**

The *eleventh hour* is that point just before a deadline, when it is almost too late to change anything – but when the situation may just be susceptible to change. In the parable it was the last chance that potential workers had of being hired by the owner of the vineyard, which high-lights the difference in references to time: this is not just before midnight, as we might take it to be, but the end of the working day. In Jesus' story, the eleventh hour is not the last chance to save the day but the door to a posi-tive, perhaps unexpected, situation: these men get to do some work after all, and are paid for a full day despite only working for the last hour. In God's plan, good can come even at the eleventh hour.

# The end is not yet

*And ye shall hear of wars and rumours of wars: see that ye be not troubled: for all these things must come to pass, but the end is not yet. For nation shall rise against nation, and*

59

*kingdom against kingdom: and there shall be famines, and*
*pestilences, and earthquakes, in divers places.*

Matthew 24:6-7

When someone says, *the end is not yet*, he or she means
that there is still time for things to change before the
final curtain. But, as the cataclysmic language of Matthew
suggests, the tone of the original saying invariably
implies not that things may improve but that worse is
yet to come. You can almost hear the speaker whisper
in hushed and fearful tones, 'You just wait. You haven't
seen anything yet.'

## Escape by the skin of your teeth
*See* **Skin of my teeth**

## Eschew
*There was a man in the land of Uz, whose name was Job;*
*and that man was perfect and upright, and one that*
*feared God, and eschewed evil.*

Job 1:1

If we hear the sound *eschew* we may well be tempted to
immediately respond by saying, 'Bless you', for it sounds
rather as if someone has just sneezed. The word tends

to be used in formal contexts these days and means 'to refuse or shun something'. This is the sense we discover when reading the description of Job at the beginning of the book of the same name. The central character was a God-fearer, noted for the fact that he turned his back on evil. With that premise at the start, the rest of the book goes on to show how, even under extreme duress, Job was true to this initial thumbnail description.

*See also* The **patience of Job**.

## Evidence

*Now when I had delivered the evidence of the purchase unto Baruch the son of Neriah, I prayed unto the LORD.*

Jeremiah 32:16

In a court of law, *evidence* is provided to act as proof of something that took place in the past. It could be a witness statement, a sample of DNA, a picture or countless other things. In the Old Testament of the King James Version *evidence* has a similar but much more limited sense. It is used to mean legal documents related to a purchase, much as the deeds to a house would be today. Jeremiah was told by God to purchase a field and when he had done so he placed the *evidence* or documents in a container for safekeeping.

# An eye for an eye

*And if any mischief follow, then thou shalt give life for life,*
*Eye for eye, tooth for tooth, hand for hand, foot for foot.*

Exodus 21:23–24

*Ye have heard that it hath been said, An eye for an eye, and*
*a tooth for a tooth: But I say unto you, That ye resist not*
*evil: but whosoever shall smite thee on thy right cheek,*
*turn to him the other also.*

Matthew 5:38–39

Anyone who has observed schoolchildren in the playground will know that they have an innate tendency to exact revenge at a higher level than the initial act of injustice. If a punch is dealt, it is generously repaid by two. If the misdemeanour in question is two kicks, then a third will be offered for good measure. *An eye for an eye* essentially means like for like. The punishment is to be directly proportional to the crime. It was the normal human thirst for revenge with interest that led to this Old Testament prohibition on letting vendettas escalate out of control. Strict guidelines were laid down to stop family feuds spiralling. Retribution was limited rather than encouraged by this law, and in his New Testament application of the principle of '*lex talionis*' (law of retaliation), Jesus takes it to a completely new level by encouraging even more restraint, instead of excessive retaliation.

# F

## Fall among thieves

*And Jesus answering said, A certain man went down from Jerusalem to Jericho, and fell among thieves, which stripped him of his raiment, and wounded him, and departed, leaving him half dead.*

Luke 10:30

To *fall among thieves* is to be thrust into a desperate situation that renders the victim vulnerable to abuse and exploitation. This is what happened to the unwitting traveller in the story of the **good Samaritan**. While on his journey, he was attacked by robbers who took everything from him and left him for dead. Had it not been for the kindly intervention of the Jews' traditional enemy, a Samaritan, he would undoubtedly have perished, far from the interest and sympathy of his fellows.

*See also* A **good Samaritan**

# Fall from grace

*Christ is become of no effect unto you, whosoever of you are justified by the law; ye are fallen from grace.*

Galatians 5:4

To *fall from grace* means to lose some high position, important post or special favour. Captains of industry, politicians and those in the public eye are frequently notable candidates for this dishonour. Very often their demise is rapid and associated with some scandal or indiscretion discovered by the media and tutted over by a disapproving audience — doubtless glad that their lives aren't subject to a similar scrutiny. Paul used the expression when speaking to the Galatians. He was deeply concerned that, having entered into the Christian faith through an understanding of God's gift of undeserved grace, the people were now trying to improve their standing by attempting to fulfil the old requirements of the Jewish legal system. Rather than seeing this as an upward step, giving an improvement in their standing, the apostle believed it to be a retrograde, downward fall.

# Fall on stony ground

*And some fell on stony ground, where it had not much earth; and immediately it sprang up, because it had no depth of earth.*

**Mark 4:5**

In Mark's telling of Jesus' famous parable of the sower he records that some of the seed *fell on stony ground*. The purpose of the story was to show different reactions to the sowing of God's word. The seed that *fell on stony ground* represented what happened when the message was ignored with barely a second thought (although interestingly, the story does have the plants growing initially). Anything, therefore, that *falls on stony ground* meets with an indifferent reception. The ideas expressed go in one ear and quickly out of the other. Almost literally, as the parable explains, these thoughts are plucked away before they have a chance to take root and grow.

# Fat of the land

*And take your father and your households, and come unto me: and I will give you the good of the land of Egypt, and ye shall eat the fat of the land.*

**Genesis 45:18**

The *fat of the land* does not refer to the increasing numbers of us who, through the medium of fast food and the genius of the internal-combustion engine, are filling ever-larger clothes in a so-called epidemic of obesity. The key to understanding this saying lies in a word found earlier in the verse in Genesis from which it comes: good. The *fat of the land* is the the best that is available, in this case specifically referring to the best of the crops and livestock, but used more broadly today. It can also be used to describe someone who enjoys a life of luxury and extravagance, perhaps acquired with very little effort on their part. Those who were invited to share in the fat of the land of Egypt certainly did very well on it. The overwhelming success of the Israelite immigrants, though, eventually led to a reaction against them, and ultimately, to the drama of suffering and escape recorded in the book of Exodus.

## The fat years and the lean years

Genesis 41

As recorded in Genesis 41, Pharaoh, the king of ancient Egypt, had two dreams. In the first, there were fat cows that were consumed by lean cows. In the second dream, a similar thing took place, but this time fat ears of corn were replaced by lean ones. The only person able to interpret the dreams was the Hebrew slave Joseph, who told the king that the different images represented *fat years* and *lean years* that were to have a great impact upon his country. The *fat years* were times of abundant harvest and food. The *lean years* were the opposite – periods of poor harvests and ensuing famine. It is for this reason that the expression is used today to describe the contrasting periods of abundance and poverty in an individual's or country's fortunes and prosperity.


## Fear and trembling

*See* **In fear and trembling**


## Feet of clay

*His legs of iron, his feet part of iron and part of clay.*

**Daniel 2:33**


When a person is said to have *feet of clay*, it means that their apparently powerful demeanour hides significant weaknesses. If this point of vulnerability is exposed and attacked, it can lead to disastrous consequences. In the book of Daniel, the all-conquering Babylonian King Nebuchadnezzar dreamt of an immense statue constructed out of a variety of precious and robust metals. It seemed indestructible. Nevertheless it had, almost literally, its Achilles heel. The feet were made of a clay and iron mixture. In his dream, Nebuchadnezzar saw a stone crash into the statue's feet, shattering them. As the feet disintegrated, so the whole structure fell to the ground and was blown away like specks of dust on a gentle breeze.

## Fight the good fight

*Fight the good fight of faith, lay hold on eternal life, whereunto thou art also called, and hast professed a good profession before many witnesses.*

**1 Timothy 6:12**

*Fight the good fight* is often used as a rallying call to those who have grown weary and exhausted in the pursuit of a worthy goal. It is intended to inspire courage, confidence and perseverance in the face of pressures that tempt to capitulation. In a letter to his close friend Timothy, Paul had been speaking of those who had lost their sense of spiritual direction under the beguiling influence of material comfort and emotional ease. He commands Timothy to turn his back on that bad, yet apparently tranquil, path, and to take up arms in the good, but clearly more perilous, path of spiritual combat.

# Filthy lucre

*For a bishop must be blameless, as the steward of God; not selfwilled, not soon angry, not given to wine, no striker, not given to filthy lucre.*

Titus 1:7

The word *lucre* and its association with terms such as *lucrative*, make many today think that it is simply an archaic word for *money*. This is not the case, for its original meaning was slightly different. *Lucre* actually means 'gain', of any sort, and the addition of the adjective 'filthy' implies that the gain spoken of is in some way tarnished. Despite what many people think, money is not anathematised in the Bible. It is people's attitudes towards it and their treatment of it that come under close scrutiny. Paul expected the highest standards from those who were to be leaders in the newly formed churches, and in this letter to Titus he speaks out against the possibility of Christian leaders being involved in any situations where they feather their own nest through dishonest, unworthy or shameful practices.

# Fire and brimstone

*Then the LORD rained upon Sodom and upon Gomorrah brimstone and fire from the LORD out of heaven.*

**Genesis 19:24**

A *fire-and-brimstone* preacher is one who not only concentrates on hell, God's wrath and judgement, but specifically does so in a manner designed to frighten and disturb the listeners. In an associated usage, a person might in anger be said to be breathing *fire and brimstone* like some ferocious dragon. The first mention of the phrase accompanies the destruction of the wicked cities of Sodom and Gomorrah. The text makes it very clear that it is God himself who is the inspiration for the mechanism of judgement which some other translations refer to as *burning sulphur*. Jesus takes up the theme in Luke 17:29, which is also echoed in Revelation where hell is described as a place with a lake of fire and brimstone. In this way, the destruction of the ancient pagan cities of Palestine becomes the symbol of the archetypal description of God's judgement on sin and its perpetrators.

# The first shall be last and the last shall be first

*But many that are first shall be last; and the last shall be first.*

Matthew 19:30

*So the last shall be first, and the first last: for many be called, but few chosen.*

Matthew 20:16

This phrase is a simple way of describing how the expected order of things has been reversed to the advantage of those who otherwise might not have anticipated it being so – for example, when someone gets pulled to the front of a queue unexpectedly. When Jesus used the phrase in consecutive parables in Matthew, he had a more serious meaning. He first explained how the rich, who were, in Jewish expectation, the primary recipients of God's blessings, would be less likely to receive them than those who had sacrificed what they had to follow him. In the next parable, it comes from the mouth of a generous farmer who challenges his employees' concern because he chose to pay everyone the same wage irrespective of the number of hours they had been contracted to work. It is a deep challenge to the human tendency to seek personal security and favour the well-to-do and worldly-wise in our dealings.

# Flee from the wrath to come

*But when he saw many of the Pharisees and Sadducees come to his baptism, he said unto them, O generation of vipers, who hath warned you to flee from the wrath to come?*

Matthew 3:7

Anyone who is advised to *flee from the wrath to come* is being told to escape some form of imminent judgement or disaster. It is one of perhaps only a few instances in the Bible where discretion is considered to be the better part of valour. When John the Baptist, who had been attracting huge crowds to his desert haunts, saw the religious leaders who had come to hear him, scepticism urged him to ask what had motivated them of all people to make the journey into the desert. He explained that the way they could flee from the coming wrath was by behaving in a way that showed they were sorry for their sins and by not relying solely on the fact of their nationalistic and religious identity.

# The flesh is weak

*See* The **spirit is willing, but the flesh is weak**

# The fleshpots of Egypt

*And the children of Israel said unto them, Would to God we*
*had died by the hand of the* Lord *in the land of Egypt,*
*when we sat by the flesh pots, and when we did eat bread*
*to the full; for ye have brought us forth into this*
*wilderness, to kill this whole assembly with hunger.*

**Exodus 16:3**

Today the word *fleshpot* lays its emphasis very much on
the *flesh* rather than the *pot*. It conjures up an image of
some seedy area, a less than salubrious bar, lap-dancing
club or similar building where bawdy entertainment is
offered and enjoyed. Everything in these locations is self-
indulgent and designed to offer maximum pleasure to
clients. The *fleshpots* of Egypt alluded to by the grumbling
Israelites did not have these sexual connotations. As they
found themselves tired, weary and above all else, hungry,
in the desert, they looked back longingly to the days when
they could sit quite happily by their cooking fires, antic-
ipating a decent meal from cooking pots that were full
of tasty meat.

# Flowers

*And if any man lie with her at all, and her flowers be upon him, he shall be unclean seven days; and all the bed whereon he lieth shall be unclean.*

**Leviticus 15:24**

Many a time I have been in a car driving through the countryside and the distinctive aroma of cow pats will waft through the windows. Upon sniffing this delicate perfume, someone invariably says 'roses'. It is a strange euphemism, but superficially no stranger than the use on occasions in the King James Version of the word *flowers* to describe the products of menstrual discharge. The English word derives not from that for the botanical feature, but from one that relates to the flow of a substance from one place to another. When understood in this way, some of the logic of using this word can be seen.

# A fly in the ointment

*Dead flies cause the ointment of the apothecary to send forth a stinking savour: so doth a little folly him that is in reputation for wisdom and honour.*

**Ecclesiastes 10:1**

Flies, and their young, are notorious for their love of everything that we find unpleasant. Unless you are keen on fishing, there can be few discoveries worse than coming across a legion of writhing maggots festering in some putrefying object. And how many times has an occasion been spoilt by the presence of a solitary fly pretending to be a yo-yo against a window pane? *A fly in the ointment* means something or someone that has managed to ruin what otherwise would have been perfectly good. To get rid of a fly from a sticky ointment is a task out of all proportion to the size of the creature because it entails removing far more of the sticky substance than you would like. That fact, combined with the possibility of germs from an unsanitary creature, renders the ointment both psychologically and biologically unclean, making it unsuitable for its intended purpose.

# A foolish virgin
## See A wise/foolish virgin

# Forbidden fruit

Genesis 3:1–17

*Forbidden fruit* refers to anything whose major appeal lies in the fact that it is out of bounds. Anyone who has seen the sign 'Keep off the grass' will appreciate the overwhelming power of the urge to do anything but – even though treading on the grass would not normally be high on their list of things to do before they die. Suddenly the aura of restriction and prohibition makes it a desirable course of action. The original *forbidden fruit* hung from the tree of the knowledge of good and evil in the Garden of Eden. While many believe it to have been an apple (clearly not a Granny Smith, as grannies hadn't been invented at that stage) there is no indication in the biblical text as to what kind of fruit was so alluring to Eve and then Adam. What is established is that the consequences of succumbing to temptation have distorted human existence and will continue to do so until the end of time.

# Found wanting

*See* **Weighed in the balance and found wanting**

# The fruit of your labours

*For to me to live is Christ, and to die is gain. But if I live in the flesh, this is the fruit of my labour: yet what I shall choose I wot not.*

Philippians 1:21–22

*The fruit of a person's labours* are the rewards he or she receives for their work. In this passage in Philippians, Paul has been explaining how he would rather be in heaven with Christ, but if that were not yet possible he would be more than glad to work on here in order to produce fruit on behalf of his Saviour.

# G

## Gay

*And ye have respect to him that weareth the gay clothing,
and say unto him, Sit thou here in a good place; and say to
the poor, Stand thou there, or sit here under my footstool.*

James 2:3

*Gay* is an interesting word, because it is a very recent
example of how words can change their meaning within
a short space of time. Even as recently as thirty years
ago it would have been understood as meaning something that was jolly or lively. Today, away from the
politically incorrect atmosphere of the playground, it is
almost exclusively used to refer to someone who is a
homosexual. The word appears only once in the King
James Version where it means 'fine' or 'rich'. James, in
the passage quoted above, is criticising Christians who
were more interested in pleasing people who appeared
to be from the upper strata of society rather than treating
everyone equally, whatever their outward appearance.

# Get thee behind me, Satan

*But he turned, and said unto Peter, Get thee behind me,*
*Satan: thou art an offence unto me: for thou savourest not*
*the things that be of God, but those that be of men.*

**Matthew 16:23**

How many times have we serial dieters joked, *Get thee behind me, Satan*, when a work colleague offers us a delicious-looking cake or a chocolate biscuit? Anyone who says this is fighting off an almost irresistible temptation. Their only hope of overcoming it is to have it removed from their presence. The phrase was twice uttered by Jesus and in much graver circumstances (although food was involved in one instance). On the first occasion (Matthew 4:10), it was as a result of a direct confrontation between himself and the devil. Satan was attempting to divert him from his appointed pathway through a series of suggestions that would have irrevocably compromised his mission. On the second occasion, although the temptation to avoid his destiny came from the mouth of his friend and follower Peter, Jesus saw behind it the same malign power that he had overcome at the start of his ministry.

# Gin

*The proud have hid a snare for me, and cords; they have spread a net by the wayside; they have set gins for me.*

**Psalm 140:5**

As far as most people are concerned, *gin* is an alcoholic beverage flavoured with juniper berries. It may also refer to the machine that separates cotton. This latter meaning gives clues as to the way it was used in the King James Version. In reality, the word *gin* was a shortened form of the word *engine*, which itself was originally derived from the word *ingenuity*, having become applied to the clever workings of machines or of products produced by the same. So one of the range of products to which it could be applied was 'snares' or 'traps'. It is in this sense that it is used, so the psalmist talks of nets and gins prepared for the express purpose of capturing him and bringing him down.

# Give up the ghost

*Then Abraham gave up the ghost, and died in a good old age, an old man, and full of years; and was gathered to his people.*

**Genesis 25:8**

As might be expected from a society that feels uncomfortable describing death, the phrase *to give up the ghost* serves us as a useful euphemism for the stark verb *to die*. It is a phrase rich in imagery – the manifestation of which can occasionally be seen in films where computer-animation wizardry allows viewers to see a corpse literally give up its inner being to the form of a ghost. The phrase can also have a less pungent meaning, being applied to any situation where someone resigns themselves to the fate that is about to befall them.

## Glory

*See* **In all his (or her) glory**

## The gnashing of teeth

*But the children of the kingdom shall be cast out into outer darkness: there shall be weeping and gnashing of teeth.*

**Matthew 8:12**

The physical action of *gnashing your teeth* is to grind the upper ones against the lower ones. This symbolises a state of anguish that reveals itself in a tangible manner. In the New Testament, the phrase is used to describe the state of extreme pain and distress that befalls those who are punished eternally by God.

## Go and do likewise

*And Jesus answering said, A certain man went down from Jerusalem to Jericho, and fell among thieves, which stripped him of his raiment, and wounded him, and departed, leaving him half dead. And by chance there came down a certain priest that way: and when he saw him, he passed by on the other side. And likewise a Levite, when he was at the place, came and looked on him, and passed by on the other side. But a certain Samaritan, as he journeyed, came where he was: and when he saw him, he had compassion on him, and went to him, and bound up his wounds, pouring in oil and wine, and set him on his own beast, and brought him to an inn, and took care of him. And on the morrow when he departed, he took out two pence, and gave them to the host, and said unto him, Take care of him; and whatsoever thou spendest more, when I come again, I will repay thee. Which now of these three, thinkest thou, was neighbour unto him that fell among the thieves? And he said, He that shewed mercy on him. Then said Jesus unto him, Go, and do thou likewise.*

Luke 10:30–37

When a lawyer asked Jesus who his neighbour was, the reply came in the form of the famous parable of the **good Samaritan**. At the conclusion of the story, Jesus turned the tables on his interrogator and asked him to answer his own question based on the account he had just heard. When the legal expert candidly admitted that the true neighbour had been the man who had offered help to the injured victim, Jesus' final comment was intensely practical. As far as he was concerned, the question of being a good neighbour wasn't merely theoretical, but intensely practical. He moved the answer away from the forum of debate and discussion to that of involvement and practical action. So he told the man to go and do likewise: to behave in the same generous, loving and undiscriminating way that the Samaritan had behaved in the parable.

## Go from strength to strength

*They go from strength to strength, every one of them in Zion appeareth before God.*

Psalm 84:7

A person or organisation that *goes from strength to strength* is one that keeps improving or becoming more successful. Psalm 84 describes pilgrims who rely totally upon God's strength. Everywhere they go is blessed through association and, rather than becoming weary or increasingly worn out, they become more and more invigorated. As the Psalm progresses it reveals that the final destination is God himself. The intention of the psalmist becomes obvious. Unlike in the physical realm where strength will peak and ultimately decline, spiritual power can go on developing and growing right up to the moment when a person faces his or her maker.


## Go the way of all the earth/flesh

*I go the way of all the earth: be thou strong therefore, and shew thyself a man.*

1 Kings 2:2

The great and incontrovertible statistic, so the morbid tell us, is that one out of every one person dies. Not just people, but animals and all living organisms are destined to perish at some point or other. If life is a journey, then the only thing every voyager has in common is that all will definitely pass to the point of final departure: death. David, in the verse highlighted above, recognised this was the case. He was about to die, or *to go the way of all flesh*.

# The golden rule

*Therefore all things whatsoever ye would that men should do to you, do ye even so to them: for this is the law and the prophets.*

Matthew 7:12

*And as ye would that men should do to you, do ye also to them likewise.*

Luke 6:31

The Bible does not contain any explicit mention of the expression *the golden rule*. The designation first appears in the nineteenth century, and has a particularly Victorian flavour. Anything that is gold is of great value and it is no surprise that this teaching which Jesus considered to encapsulate the essence of the law and the prophets should be assigned such great worth. The exact nature of the rule is variously defined in everyday speech along the lines of, 'Do as you would be done by', or 'Do unto others as you would have them do unto you.' This golden rule appears at the end of the Sermon on the Mount and was considered by Jesus himself to be the summary of all that he had been teaching in the preceding chapters of Matthew's Gospel.

# A good Samaritan

*And Jesus answering said, A certain man went down from Jerusalem to Jericho, and fell among thieves, which stripped him of his raiment, and wounded him, and departed, leaving him half dead. And by chance there came down a certain priest that way: and when he saw him, he passed by on the other side. And likewise a Levite, when he was at the place, came and looked on him, and passed by on the other side. But a certain Samaritan, as he journeyed, came where he was: and when he saw him, he had compassion on him, and went to him, and bound up his wounds, pouring in oil and wine, and set him on his own beast, and brought him to an inn, and took care of him. And on the morrow when he departed, he took out two pence, and gave them to the host, and said unto him, Take care of him; and whatsoever thou spendest more, when I come again, I will repay thee. Which now of these three, thinkest thou, was neighbour unto him that fell among the thieves? And he said, He that shewed mercy on him. Then said Jesus unto him, Go, and do thou likewise.*

Luke 10:30–37

A *good Samaritan* is anyone who helps another person in a time of crisis. The expression does not actually appear in the Bible text itself, but springs from one of the most well-known of Jesus' parables. His story centres on an unknown inhabitant of the region of Samaria who, coming across the victim of a particularly vicious robbery, does everything within his power to assist the injured man. Familiarity with the expression hides the fact that to a Jew the concept of a good Samaritan was non-existent. The two people groups had little in common other than mutual contempt and 'good' was the last adjective a Jew might have used to describe a Samaritan. Jesus told the parable to explain the true meaning of the word *neighbour*. His deliberate choice of a despised Samaritan capable of showing a compassion that transcended national and religious barriers, would have both appalled his critics and appealed to his followers.

Other expressions that derive from this parable and have become part of our language include: **Fall among thieves; Go and do likewise; Pass by on the other side**.


## Good works

*Now there was at Joppa a certain disciple named Tabitha, which by interpretation is called Dorcas: this woman was full of good works and almsdeeds which she did.*

**Acts 9:36**

*Good works* are acts of kindness that are intended to help

improve the lot of those in difficult situations or who have special needs. In Acts 9:36 the Christian lady, Tabitha, was highly regarded because of the continual support and assistance she gave the poor and the widows. She was following Christ's words in the Sermon on the Mount when Jesus says to his followers, 'Let your light so shine before others, that they may see your good works, and glorify your Father, who is in heaven' (Matthew 5:16).

# H

## Halt

*And if thy foot offend thee, cut it off: it is better for thee to enter halt into life, than having two feet to be cast into hell, into the fire that never shall be quenched.*

**Mark 9:45**

Any aficionado of war stories, whether on film or in book form, will know that the word *Halt* is usually followed by the question, 'Who goes there?' It is a command designed to stop a person in his or her tracks. In the King James Version, though, it is used to describe a range of activities that are all associated with the inability to walk normally. So it can mean 'lame', 'crippled' or 'limping'. In the verse from Mark, Jesus is explaining that it would be better to limp into heaven as a result of self-mutilation than end up in hell – though the practical outworking of this is more likely to involve spiritual than physical self-sacrifice.

# Harmless as doves

*See* **Wise as serpents, and harmless as doves**

# Hate

*If any man come to me, and hate not his father, and mother, and wife, and children, and brethren, and sisters, yea, and his own life also, he cannot be my disciple.*

**Luke 14:26**

*And he went in also unto Rachel, and he loved also Rachel more than Leah, and served with him yet seven other years. And when the LORD saw that Leah was hated, he opened her womb: but Rachel was barren.*

**Genesis 29:30–31**

If we *hate* someone or something it means that we positively dislike them. The King James Version also gives another meaning to the word. On occasions, it can mean only 'to love less'. When Jesus speaks in Luke 14 he is saying that a person's love for him should be greater than their love for anyone else. The passage in Genesis shows how, when God realised that Jacob loved his wife Leah less than his other wife Rachel, he compensated for this by blessing her with children while Rachel remained unable to conceive.

# The heat of the day

*See* **Bear the burden and heat of the day**

# Hewers of wood and drawers of water

*And the princes said unto them, Let them live; but let them be hewers of wood and drawers of water unto all the congregation; as the princes had promised them.*

Joshua 9:21

The expression *hewers of wood and drawers of water* describes people who perform laborious menial tasks. Its biblical roots lie in the book of Joshua which describes the invasion of Palestine following the Israelites' forty-year wanderings in the desert. One of the indigenous people groups in the land, the Gibeonites, heard of the all-conquering power of Joshua's army and, fearing they would be annihilated along with other indigenous groups, embarked on a plan of deception. Some of their number pretended to be travellers from a distant land and tricked Joshua into signing a mutual pact of non-aggression. After all, why shouldn't he sign such an agreement with a far-off people, who would be of little threat to him? Later, the Israelites discovered they had been deceived, but could not revoke the peace treaty. What Joshua was able to do, however, was punish the Gibeonites by consigning them to a life of servitude. In exchange for their survival, the Gibeonites became wood cutters and water carriers in the service of the invaders, so the same sense of servitude and of people confined to doing lowly tasks carries over to the meaning of this phrase today.

## Hide your light under a bushel

*Neither do men light a candle, and put it under a bushel, but on a candlestick; and it giveth light unto all that are in the house.*

Matthew 5:15

A *bushel* is a container which was used in Israel to measure out quantities of flour and other foodstuffs. If you *hide your light under a bushel* it means either that you are overly modest about your skills, abilities or achievements, or that you hang back from using or speaking about them even when the possibility of doing so presents itself. When Jesus spoke these words, he conjured up the nonsensical idea of someone taking the trouble to light a candle (which was a precious and costly item), only then to cover its light under an object that would completely obscure any illumination it gave out. Candles were made to bring light, and any use that hindered this capacity would be absurd.

# Holier than thou

*Which say, Stand by thyself, come not near to me; for I am*
*holier than thou. These are a smoke in my nose, a fire that*
*burneth all the day.*

**Isaiah 65:5**

Anyone who has a *holier-than-thou* attitude behaves in a self-righteous manner. They consider themselves to be spiritually or morally superior to everyone else. In Isaiah, where the phrase originates, the expression is used to describe people who have little regard for the demands of the Jewish law. Yet when others attempt to reproach them, they claim the moral high ground and order them away. How could such wonderfully upright people contaminate themselves by contact with those who don't match up to their exacting standards?

# Holy of holies

*And thou shalt put the mercy seat upon the ark of the*
*testimony in the most holy place.*

**Exodus 26:34**

In ancient Israel the *holy of holies* (or Most Holy Place) was the most special part of the Temple or, before that was built, the tabernacle. Inside was the Ark of the

95

Covenant, the container for the tablets of stone on which the Ten Commandments were written. A thick curtain separated the holy of holies from the rest of the Temple and it was out of bounds to everyone except the high priest, and even he could enter there only once a year. Consequently, the expression describes any location that is considered to be especially holy, although it has lost much of its sense of awe, and is frequently used to describe, in jest, any location where entrance is restricted to 'important' people only.


## A house divided against itself

*And Jesus knew their thoughts, and said unto them, Every kingdom divided against itself is brought to desolation; and every city or house divided against itself shall not stand.*

Matthew 12:25

If a family, group, club or organisation is in a state of internal strife and quarrelling, an outside observer may remark that it is *a house divided against itself*. Such a state of affairs is more often than not a recipe for disaster. When Jesus used the expression, he was responding to the accusation of the Pharisees who claimed that he was cooperating with Satan in order to exorcise demons. He pointed out the absurdity of their logic. His enemies considered demonic activity to be the work of Satan, so why would Satan wish to limit this expression of his influence by encouraging Jesus to release people from his evil power? If that were the case, Satan would be on a mission of self-destruction.

## How the mighty are fallen

*The beauty of Israel is slain upon thy high places: how are the mighty fallen! How are the mighty fallen in the midst of the battle! O Jonathan, thou wast slain in thine high places. How are the mighty fallen, and the weapons of war perished!*

2 Samuel 1:19, 25, 27

When a famous person, or some seemingly impregnable economic institution undergoes a dramatic reverse in fortune, tongues may well begin to wag, whispering *How are the mighty fallen*! The comment is usually tongue-in-cheek and lacks the passion and intensity surrounding the circumstances where it appears in the Bible. Three times in 2 Samuel 1, David, Israel's king-in-waiting, cries out this mournful lament when he learns of the news of the deaths of Jonathan and his father, King Saul. The occasion has double poignancy

97

in that Jonathan was David's dear friend and supporter in the royal court. In addition, David himself had ample justification and opportunity to kill Saul, who had hounded him relentlessly. Nevertheless he had repeatedly refused to lift a finger against the man appointed by God as king over the nation.

# I

## Impotent

*In these lay a great multitude of impotent folk, of blind, halt, withered, waiting for the moving of the water.*

John 5:3

Most people, if asked what *impotent* meant, would think in terms of a male lacking the ability to perform sexual intercourse. The other common use would relate to lacking strength or power to do something. In the story from John 5 the meaning of the word is just used generally to mean 'ill' or 'illness'. It was a generic word used to describe unspecified ailments.

## In all his (or her) glory

*And yet I say unto you, That even Solomon in all his glory was not arrayed like one of these.*

Matthew 6:29

When we talk of a person *in all his* (or *her*) *glory*, we are referring to the individual's wonderful appearance or beauty, though it might also be used in referring to excellence in a specific area, so might include an athlete's gold medal run, a musician's virtuosity or a painter's artistic talent. The original *glory* to which Jesus was referring was that of great King Solomon whose fame, achievements and court were heralded throughout the world. The point he was making was that, despite their obvious splendour, Solomon and the trappings of his reign were as nothing compared to the simple yet amazing beauty of a flower created by God.

## In fear and trembling

*Wherefore, my beloved, as ye have always obeyed, not as in my presence only, but now much more in my absence, work out your own salvation with fear and trembling.*

**Philippians 2:12**

Which of us has not gone into a headteacher's study or our manager's office, or else answered a phone call in the middle of the night, without a sense of dread at what may be about to happen? This apprehension helps us grasp some of the sense of the expression *fear and trembling* that describes a sensation of anxiety and trepidation. Paul used the phrase when reminding the disciples in Philippi not to treat their salvation in a casual, flippant manner, but to approach it in a deep and serious way.

## In the twinkling of an eye

*Behold, I show you a mystery; We shall not all sleep, but we shall all be changed, in a moment, in the twinkling of an eye, at the last trump: for the trumpet shall sound, and the dead shall be raised incorruptible, and we shall be changed.*

1 Corinthians 15:51–52

If an eye twinkles it is not because of anything in the eye itself, but rather because of the influence of light on it. It is light, the most rapid of all natural phenomena, that gives the expression its sense of speed. Consequently when something happens *in the twinkling of an eye*, it occurs, or appears to occur, incredibly quickly – if not instantly. In the New Testament, Paul uses the phrase to describe the moment of transformation of a person's earthly body to the new resurrection one when Jesus Christ returns, and we now use it for anything that happens with unexpected or extraordinary speed.

## In word and deed

*My little children, let us not love in word, neither in tongue; but in deed and in truth.*

1 John 3:18

John's call to love *in word and deed* recorded in this his first letter, communicated his desire for Christians to show their love practically, not just through their speech. And so today when we say *in word and deed* we mean 'not just by what we say, but also by what we do.' The expression is not an exact rendition of this quotation from John's letter or of the similar one in 2 Corinthians 10:11, but it encapsulates the essence of the meaning in both instances.

## Incontinent

*Without natural affection, trucebreakers, false accusers, incontinent, fierce, despisers of those that are good*

2 Timothy 3:3

Anyone who is described as *incontinent* today is someone who is unable to control his or her bladder and/or bowels. A quick glance at the text above makes us appreciate the unlikelihood of it having held the same meaning when the King James Version was penned.

Indeed at that time the word *incontinent* meant lacking in self-control in the general rather than the specific medical sense.

# J

## Jacob's ladder

*And he dreamed, and behold a ladder set up on the earth,
and the top of it reached to heaven: and behold the angels
of God ascending and descending on it.*

Genesis 28:12

In the narrative recorded in Genesis, Jacob, fleeing from
his brother Esau after stealing his birthright, has a
memorable dream in which he sees angels moving up
and down a ladder or stairway that goes into heaven.
These steps have given rise to two different usages. The
plant, Jacob's ladder (*Polemonium caeruleum*), derives its
name from the interlacing light green leaves that give
it the appearance of a ladder. The other use refers to a
ship's ladder made from a flexible material such as rope
or steel with inflexible rungs made from wood or metal.
As such it is easily rolled out over the ship's side so that
people may transfer to and from smaller vessels that have
drawn alongside.

# Jangling

*From which some having swerved have turned aside unto vain jangling.*

1 Timothy 1:6

Jangling is what wind chimes do — it can be especially wearing on the nerves as they initially delight then slowly begin to irritate with their incessant tinkling and metallic clanking. While the sense of the word in the King James Version has some elements of this, it actually refers to pointless, meaningless speech. It was against such idle tittle-tattle that Paul was warning his readers.

# Jeremiah

A *Jeremiah* is a gloomy, pessimistic person whose outlook on life and society is extremely negative and depressing. In the Bible, the prophet Jeremiah is sometimes considered the archetypal prophet of doom. His message was unpalatable and full of foreboding, predicting judgement and distress. Coupled with his message was his bizarre lifestyle which saw him among other things, walking the streets, not with a sandwich board announcing 'The end is nigh', which would have seemed lighthearted for him, but with a yoke across his neck. He was mocked, imprisoned, thrown into a pit and left for dead — experiences that would have taken the joy out of most people. Indeed, at times in his prophecy he comes across as angry or bitter, but he was nevertheless unwilling to sacrifice his preaching on the altar of popularity.

## Jeroboam

*And the man Jeroboam was a mighty man of valour: and Solomon seeing the young man that he was industrious, he made him ruler over all the charge of the house of Joseph.*

1 Kings 11:28

*And he shall give Israel up because of the sins of Jeroboam, who did sin, and who made Israel to sin.*

1 Kings 14:16

Wine connoisseurs will know that a *jeroboam* is a large bottle which holds the same amount of wine as four standard bottles. It is also known as a 'double magnum'. King Jeroboam was both a 'mighty man' and a bad king who led his people in his wicked ways. *Jeroboam* therefore seems an apt name to give to a bottle that is big and whose contents are capable of leading their consumer into wild and potentially sinful ways.

Other bottle sizes named after Old Testament figures

include: the *rehoboam*, six standard wine bottles – named after Rehoboam, a son of Solomon, the last king of the united Israel and the first king of Judah. His name means 'expansion of the people'; the *methuselah*, eight standard wine bottles – after the patriarch Methuselah, who lived to 969 years (Genesis 5:27); the *salmanazar*, twelve standard wine bottles – after Shalmaneser, king of Assyria (2 Kings 17:3); the *balthazar*, 16 standard wine bottles – after King Belshazzar of Babylon, who drank wine at the great feast (Daniel 5:1); and the *nebuchadnezzar*, 20 standard wine bottles – after King Nebuchadnezzar of Babylon.

## Jezebel

*And it came to pass, as if it had been a light thing for him to walk in the sins of Jeroboam the son of Nebat, that he took to wife Jezebel the daughter of Ethbaal king of the Zidonians, and went and served Baal, and worshipped him.*

1 Kings 16:31

*( . . . For it was so, when Jezebel cut off the prophets of the LORD, that Obadiah took an hundred prophets, and hid them by fifty in a cave, and fed them with bread and water.) Was it not told my lord what I did when Jezebel slew the prophets of the LORD, how I hid an hundred men of*

*the LORD's prophets by fifty in a cave, and fed them with
bread and water? Now therefore send, and gather to me all
Israel unto mount Carmel, and the prophets of Baal four
hundred and fifty, and the prophets of the groves four
hundred, which eat at Jezebel's table.*

1 Kings 18:4, 13, 19

*Jezebel* was the wife of Ahab, king of Israel. During her
reign of influence she was responsible for luring her
husband and subjects away from worshipping Israel's
God. Instead she seduced them into following the foreign
god, Baal. She ordered the death of many true prophets,
replacing them with those of her own god. One of her
most unpleasant moves was securing the vineyard of
Naboth for her husband (1 Kings 21). When Naboth
refused to sell his land she bribed men to falsely accuse
Naboth of blasphemy against God (hardly evenhanded,
given her own religious beliefs). He was found guilty
and consequently executed. When the prophet Elijah
condemned her for this, she tried to kill him too, but
he fled into hiding. Her end was a violent one, as Elijah
had predicted. She was ejected from a palace window and
trampled to death. Given the details of her wicked,
callous life, it comes as no surprise that when someone
is called a *Jezebel* today they are condemned as a thor-
oughly immoral, unscrupulous woman.

# A Job's comforter

*Then Job answered and said, I have heard many such things: miserable comforters are ye all.*

Job 16:1

When things are going badly, we all want reliable friends who will stand by us, sympathise with us and offer us support in the midst of troubles. Nobody wants *a Job's comforter*, though. This person is one who comes alongside but only makes us feel worse than before. Whether intentionally or otherwise, he or she manages to rub salt into our wounds so our grim situation appears even more gloomy. The original *Job's comforters* were three men who attempted to help Job, a good man who had been overtaken by a series of terrible misfortunes. Their well-meaning moralising and attempts at helping him understand the possible reasons for his afflictions did nothing to assist him. In his frustration he called them 'miserable comforters'.

*See also* The **patience of Job**.

# Jonah

Sadly, a *Jonah* is not the sort of person many people would wish to have as a friend, for a Jonah is someone who is thought to bring bad luck. When reading the account of this prophet in the Old Testament, it is not hard to see why. Called by God to preach to the inhabitants of the city of Nineveh, instead he went in the opposite direction and boarded a ship to Tarshish. While at sea, the boat was caught up in a terrifying storm. The superstitious sailors drew lots to ascertain which of those on board was responsible for bringing such a dreadful storm on them. The lot fell on Jonah who acknowledged that it was his fault that they were all caught up in such dire straits. He urged them to throw him into the sea. No sooner had they done so than the gale dissipated. The story continues in that he is swallowed by a great fish (traditionally, a whale). Inside the fish, Jonah prays, and he is spat out onto the dry land. Jonah chapter 3 records his obedience to God's second call to him.

## A jot or tittle

*For verily I say unto you, Till heaven and earth pass, one jot or one tittle shall in no wise pass from the law, till all be fulfilled.*

**Matthew 5:18**

The word *jot* comes from the original Greek, *iota*, the smallest letter in the alphabet, which was translated by early English translators as *iote*. Over time this became the word 'jot' which we retain today. The word *tittle* was chosen by Tyndale. It stood for the Greek word for *horn*, which in the context of writing was applied to any small addition to a letter, such as a serif, a stroke or a point. This combination of two words, both meaning 'small', have thus come to represent the minutest part of anything. What Jesus meant in the Sermon on the Mount was that not even the least significant part of the law could be ignored until all of it had been fulfilled.

## Judas

Of all the characters of history, not just the Bible, *Judas* has come to symbolise the ultimate in treachery. His name is associated with anyone who is a traitor to a friend. Judas was one of the original twelve apostles, hand-picked by Jesus to be with him and learn about his teaching. Yet, despite his closeness to Christ, Judas eventually chose to betray him to the Jewish authorities in exchange for money (*see* **Thirty pieces of silver**). A meeting place was chosen at which Judas would hand him over to them. In order that the wrong person would not be arrested, Judas told his co-conspirators that he would kiss Jesus to indicate who he was (Matthew 26:48–49). Consequently a *Judas kiss* is a false sign of love or affection designed to hide sentiments of duplicity. Other *Judas*-related phrases include the *Judas slit*, which is a small hole through which a guard, for example, might keep an eye on a prisoner. And a *Judas tree* is one of the genus *Cercis*, and is so named because it is thought that Judas, overcome with shame, hanged himself on a tree from this family.

## Judge not, that ye be not judged

*Judge not, that ye be not judged.*

Matthew 7:1

*Judge not, and ye shall not be judged: condemn not, and ye shall not be condemned: forgive, and ye shall be forgiven.*

Luke 6:37

This salutary piece of advice means we must not be quick to condemn other people, for if we do, others may one day apply the same sort of criteria to us. Jesus spoke this saying in the Sermon on the Mount as a warning against those who easily saw other people's faults and errors whilst being oblivious to their own.

# K

## Kill the fatted calf

*And bring hither the fatted calf, and kill it; and let us eat, and be merry: for this my son was dead, and is alive again; he was lost, and is found. And they began to be merry.*

Luke 15:23–24

The phrase *kill the fatted calf* means to spare no expense in providing entertainment for an honoured guest. It appears in Jesus' much loved parable of the **prodigal son**. When the boy's father greeted his errant son on his return from self-imposed exile, he ordered his servants to prepare the fatted calf for the celebratory feast. The fatted calf was an animal that had been specially fed in readiness for eating. So great was the father's joy at seeing his son back home that he considered only the best of his produce fitting for such a joyful occasion.

## Know not what they do

*Then said Jesus, Father, forgive them; for they know not
what they do. And they parted his raiment, and cast lots.*

Luke 23:34

If we accuse another person of *knowing not what they
do*, we are pointing out that they are acting more out of
ignorance than malice. When he was dying on the cross,
Jesus uttered seven last 'words' or 'phrases'. One of these
was 'they know not what they do'. By this he meant that
those responsible for his execution were unaware of the
deep significance of what they were doing. The authorities believed Jesus to be a blasphemer, defying their
religious laws and offending God. As far as they were
concerned, they were simply applying the law against
him. Jesus knew that they hadn't really understood who
he was or what he had come to accomplish.

## Know them by their fruits

*Ye shall know them by their fruits. Do men gather grapes
of thorns, or figs of thistles? Even so every good tree
bringeth forth good fruit; but a corrupt tree bringeth forth
evil fruit. A good tree cannot bring forth evil fruit, neither
can a corrupt tree bring forth good fruit. Every tree that*

*bringeth not forth good fruit is hewn down, and cast into the fire. Wherefore by their fruits ye shall know them.*

**Matthew 7:16–20**

*To know someone by his* (or *her*) *fruits* means to assess who a person really is based on the tangible evidence that they produce in their lives. Jesus used the expression in the Sermon on the Mount with the precise logic that good trees produce good fruit while bad trees produce bad fruit. He knew that his listeners would understand his analogy and so he urged them to apply the same standard when assessing those who were claiming to speak on God's behalf.

# L

## The labourer is worthy of his hire

*And in the same house remain, eating and drinking such things as they give: for the labourer is worthy of his hire. Go not from house to house.*

Luke 10:7

If we want to say that a worker deserves to be rewarded for the work that he or she has done, we may use this biblical phrase, *the labourer is worthy of his hire*. The words came from the mouth of Jesus when he was advising a group of his disciples how to behave when they went out and about on his behalf. He was telling them not to be embarrassed or reluctant to receive hospitality if people were kind enough to offer it. What they were doing was a noble calling and so it was entirely reasonable that they should expect some form of compensation or reward for it.

# A lamb to the slaughter

*See* **Led like a lamb to the slaughter**

# A land flowing with milk and honey

*And I am come down to deliver them out of the hand of the Egyptians, and to bring them up out of that land unto a good land and a large, unto a land flowing with milk and honey; unto the place of the Canaanites, and the Hittites, and the Amorites, and the Perizzites, and the Hivites, and the Jebusites.*

**Exodus 3:8**

With the possible exception of the lactose-intolerant and those allergic to bee stings, most people would love to be in a land flowing with milk and honey, though it might get overwhelming after a while. But the phrase doesn't refer literally to a place inhabited by herds of cows and buzzing hives, rather to a state of abundance, joy and peace where nothing can ruin our hopes and expectations. The original land which was so described was Canaan, the Promised Land that God had promised first to Abraham and then to Moses when he appeared to him in the burning bush. After their escape from Egypt, spies went to investigate the land (Numbers 13), and they confirmed what God had promised – it was indeed flowing with milk and honey, and replete with wonderful fruit. Sadly for them, the Israelites failed to take possession of the land at that time because they feared its inhabitants, but, after wandering in the desert for forty years they finally settled in the place God had intended them to possess and enjoy.

*See also* The **promised land**.

## The land of Nod

*And Cain went out from the presence of the LORD, and dwelt in the land of Nod, on the east of Eden.*

**Genesis 4:16**

If a person is in the land of Nod he or she is, in fact, asleep. The location is described in Genesis and is the place where Cain lived after he had murdered his brother Abel. It is unclear how the region became associated with sleep and the phrase we use probably owes more to an English pun on the idea of someone nodding off. In Hebrew, *nod* means 'wandering' rather than anything connected with sleep.

# The last shall be first

*See* The **first shall be last and the last shall be first**

# The law of the Medes and Persians

*Now, O king, establish the decree, and sign the writing, that it be not changed, according to the law of the Medes and Persians, which altereth not.*

**Daniel 6:8**

The *law of the Medes and Persians* is used to refer to an unalterable law that has to be followed to the smallest detail and cannot be revoked in any way. The expression appears in Daniel on the lips of enemies of the main character of the book as they dupe the king into passing an edict they knew would entrap the godly Israelite. Knowing the king held a high opinion of Daniel, they urged him to create a law which prohibited prayer other than to the king himself. They were aware that once the law came onto the statute books it could not be repealed. This left the king with no chance of bailing out his friend Daniel when he realised that the law was targeted against him – although since God saves Daniel from the lion's den, the overall message of the story is that, in the final analysis, God's power surpasses even the unchangeable laws of the Medes and the Persians.

# A law unto themselves

*For when the Gentiles, which have not the law, do by nature the things contained in the law, these, having not the law, are a law unto themselves.*

**Romans 2:14**

Contrary to expectations, the phrase *a law unto themselves* did not arise when teenagers were first discovered, nor despite its obvious aptness, do its origins lie in descriptions of members of parliament. The expression is used today to describe people who do what they think best, irrespective of the norms and expectations of society and those around them. It conjures up the idea of unyielding, headstrong individuals whose self-belief far outweighs any other considerations and who refuse to conform to normal laws and regulations. The words were originally penned by the apostle Paul in Romans as he attempted to explain that non-Jews (or those without the benefits of the Jewish law), nevertheless still had within themselves a drive to follow moral laws – so that the way we use this phrase is in direct opposition to its first use.

# Lean years

*See* The **fat years and the lean years**

## Leaven the whole lump

*Your glorying is not good. Know ye not that a little leaven leaveneth the whole lump?*

1 Corinthians 5:6

If something *leavens the whole lump*, the inference is that a very small constituent of the whole has nevertheless had the effect of changing and influencing the complete entity. The allusion comes from the domestic sphere of baking. A small amount of leaven or yeast is responsible for making the bread rise – its abilities are seemingly out of all proportion to its minuscule size. While the use of yeast, for bread-lovers at least, is seen as a positive thing, in his use of the illustration in 1 Corinthians, Paul emphasises the fact that small things can have disproportionate, negative, destructive influences too.

## Led like a lamb to the slaughter

*He was oppressed, and he was afflicted, yet he opened not his mouth: he is brought as a lamb to the slaughter, and as a sheep before her shearers is dumb, so he openeth not his mouth.*

Isaiah 53:7

*The place of the scripture which he read was this, He was led as a sheep to the slaughter; and like a lamb dumb before his shearer, so opened he not his mouth.*

**Acts 8:32**

The idea of being *led like a lamb to the slaughter* conjures up the dreadful imagery of unwitting, uncomplaining Jews being led to their deaths in a gas chamber during the Second World War. It captures the innocence, meekness and helplessness of the victims in the face of some savage atrocity. Just as a sheep may well offer no resistance to the fate that is about to befall it, so the suffering servant described by Isaiah in chapter 53 surrendered quietly to his destiny. In the New Testament the evangelist Philip meets an Ethiopian who is reading the same passage. Philip explains that the prophet is talking about Jesus.

## Your left hand does not know what your right hand is doing

*Take heed that ye do not your alms before men, to be seen of them: otherwise ye have no reward of your Father which is in heaven. But when thou doest alms, let not thy left hand know what thy right hand doeth.*

**Matthew 6:1, 3**

If you receive two apparently conflicting letters from one company, you might say that *the left hand doesn't know what the right hand is doing*. What this means is that within an entity that is supposed to be acting as a single unit there seems to be very little inner communication. The comment is not meant to be complimentary, but critical. This is in contrast to its use by Jesus in the Sermon on the Mount. He was explaining how, when a person went about giving to charity he or she should not be ostentatious. Instead, giving was to be done in such a quiet, unobtrusive way that not even different parts of the same body should know what was going on. This is clearly impossible, but the use of hyperbole forcibly emphasises the point he was making.

## Let the dead bury their dead

*And another of his disciples said unto him, Lord, suffer me first to go and bury my father. But Jesus said unto him, Follow me; and let the dead bury their dead.*

**Matthew 8:21–22**

There is nothing spooky or ghoulish about this expression. If someone remarks, *let the dead bury their dead*, what he or she means is that the past is best left as it is. There is enough to be getting on with in the present and the future. Jesus uttered the saying when one of his disciples asked if he might be excused from following him to attend to the burial of his father. It is unlikely that the man's father had recently died. Some commentators suspect that the request for a delay was rooted in an expectation that a child, of whatever age, was not free to leave the family sphere until released by the death of his father. Thus the man may have been asking to delay his discipleship for an indefinite period, whereas Jesus expected it to begin at once.

## The letter of the law/the letter that kills

*Not that we are sufficient of ourselves to think any thing as of ourselves; but our sufficiency is of God; who also hath made us able ministers of the new testament; not of the letter, but of the spirit: for the letter killeth, but the spirit giveth life.*

**2 Corinthians 3:5–6**

Both these expressions derive from the same passage in 2 Corinthians. To do something according to *the letter of the law* means to strictly adhere to the exact meaning of a particular piece of legislation. It is frequently compared to what is known as *the spirit of the law*, referring to the general intention of a legal document. *The letter killeth* is a phrase that refers to the effect of the Old Testament law. While the law is good in itself, the inevitable failure of the Jews to live up to its exacting standards led to Paul's regarding it as an instrument of death and condemnation. He compared it unfavourably with the Spirit who gives life and power, enabling all who depend on his strength to follow the true law of God.

## Light

*And they gave him threescore and ten pieces of silver out of the house of Baal-berith, wherewith Abimelech hired vain and light persons, which followed him.*

Judges 9:4

*Light* is a word that scarcely needs explanation. It has many uses in modern English, ranging from something that is not heavy to a device that illuminates. On a couple of occasions in the King James Version, though, its meaning differs significantly from what we might expect today. It is used to refer to people who are worthless, reckless or wanton, the kind that mothers would be horrified at if their sons or daughters were to bring them home for tea. In Judges, when Abimelech hired men who became his followers, they were the original motley crew: unsavoury men who could only find comfort in the company of those whose nature was as unpleasant as their own.

## Like a thief in the night

*For yourselves know perfectly that the day of the Lord so cometh as a thief in the night. For when they shall say, Peace and safety; then sudden destruction cometh upon them, as travail upon a woman with child; and they shall not escape.*

**1 Thessalonians 5:2–3**

Something that takes place *like a thief in the night* occurs without warning, taking everyone by surprise. In Thessalonians, the apostle Paul uses the phrase to describe the unexpected arrival of the day of the Lord. If we knew the exact time that a thief would try to enter our house, we would be prepared for it. Paul is saying that Christ's second coming will come unexpectedly; we are reminded of Christ's call to be constantly alert and ready for his return (Matthew 24:42–44).

## A lion in the path/way

*The slothful man saith, There is a lion in the way; a lion is in the streets.*

**Proverbs 26:13**

If a friend says there is *a lion in the way*, what he or she means is that they are facing an obstruction they feel is too difficult to pass so they have opted to do nothing instead. Very often the excuse is as much imaginary as real, and some people become proficient at being able to observe the king of the jungle at any opportunity. Of such people it might be more appropriate to say that they are more interested in enjoying a lie-in, rather than being good at spotting a lion! This was the background to the observation of a lazy person in the book of Proverbs where the saying originates.

## The lion/wolf shall lie down with the lamb

*The wolf also shall dwell with the lamb, and the leopard shall lie down with the kid; and the calf and the young lion and the fatling together; and a little child shall lead them.*

**Isaiah 11:6**

The time when *the lion shall lie down with the lamb* refers to a peaceful, prosperous future when even traditional enemies are reconciled and the prey is able to live fearlessly alongside the predator. The phrase can be used to describe the situation when two countries – especially where one is seen as the dominating, intimidating power

– settle their differences and co-exist amicably. The wording is not an exact rendition of Isaiah's prophetic statement, but it captures the spirit of the passage in which he speaks of a future promising an outlook of eternal peace for the world.

## The lions' den

Daniel 6

No one – not even a zoo keeper – would ever wish to be thrown into *the lions' den*. It is a place of danger and to be avoided at all costs. Anyone who has found himself or herself in this situation has been thrust into a predicament of extreme peril where the odds against survival are overwhelming and there is no apparent means of escape. All that awaits them is a gruesome and terrible end. This was the lot of Daniel in the Old Testament, who defied the orders of the ruler of Babylon and continued his practice of public prayer. His punishment was to be shut up for a night with some ravenous lions. He was thrown into their den and a stone moved over the entrance hole. To the astonishment of all – not least his accusers – Daniel survived his ordeal, thanks to the intervention of God's angel.

# The love of money is the root of all evil

*But they that will be rich fall into temptation and a snare, and into many foolish and hurtful lusts, which drown men in destruction and perdition. For the love of money is the root of all evil: which while some coveted after, they have erred from the faith, and pierced themselves through with many sorrows.*

1 Timothy 6:9–10

If you received a pound for every time someone misquotes this verse from the Bible, you might be at risk of falling foul of their misquotation's sentiment! What people often do is leave out the first three words, wrongly rendering the phrase as *money is the root of all evil*. In actual fact, Paul nowhere condemns money in itself. What he does speak out against is the love of it. Other translations of the verse say not that the love of money is the root of all that is wicked, but that it is the precursor to many manifestations of evil.

# M

## Magnify

*And Mary said, My soul doth magnify the Lord.*

Luke 1:46

After her visit from the angel informing her of the anticipated birth of Jesus, Mary broke into the famous poem, the *Magnificat*. This name, used in the *Book of Common Prayer*, comes from the opening lines in Latin *Magnificat anima mea Dominum* ('My soul doth magnify the Lord'). The meaning of *magnify* in this instance is 'to give thanks or praise to God' and is rarely used today outside religious worship. Most people would limit its use to those situations when an image is enlarged by the use of specially prepared glass. A possible link today between the two concepts might be when in contemporary language someone or something is 'bigged up' or made to seem more important.

# Make bricks without straw

*Ye shall no more give the people straw to make brick, as heretofore: let them go and gather straw for themselves.*

Exodus 5:7

If you are unfortunate enough to be asked to *make bricks without straw*, you are being expected to do a job of work without the necessary materials, and possibly also under unrealistic circumstances. This was the lot of the Israelite slaves in Egypt. When Moses, their potential liberator, approached Pharaoh, asking him to release his work-force, he refused. Instead, he made life even harder for them by not providing them with the straw that was vital for their brick-making. He was not, as the popular saying implies, suggesting they build without straw, but rather that in addition to their construction work, they would also have to go out and gather the straw that was integral to their labours.

# Mammon

*See* **Serve God and Mammon**

# A man after my own heart

*But now thy kingdom shall not continue: the LORD hath sought him a man after his own heart, and the LORD hath commanded him to be captain over his people, because thou hast not kept that which the LORD commanded thee.*

1 Samuel 13:14

Although today we are more likely to hear the expression *after my own heart*, the original quotation says, 'after his own heart', that is God's heart. In 1 Samuel 13 King Saul had just offered a sacrifice to God and might have expected the Almighty to have been pleased with him for having done so. He couldn't have been more wrong. No sooner had he finished than the prophet Samuel arrived and reprimanded him, effectively announcing that because of Saul's disobedience God had found a replacement king: one who would think and act as God would like – someone *after his own heart*. Composers of popular love songs have not been slow to pick up on the imagery: the notion of two people whose ways, habits and customs are so in tune with each other that everything they do is perfectly synchronised. Saul had started off well, but had come to rely upon his own heart rather than listening to the steady beat of God's heart.

# Man shall not live by bread alone

*And he humbled thee, and suffered thee to hunger, and fed thee with manna, which thou knewest not, neither did thy fathers know; that he might make thee know that man doth not live by bread only, but by every word that proceedeth out of the mouth of the LORD doth man live.*

**Deuteronomy 8:3**

These words often come with a sense of pious rebuke. They may be a friendly warning shot across the bows — from a friend who, by implication, has no such fixation. 'There are other things in life besides food, football or who's been seen going out with who.' This closely reflects the sense that first appears in Deuteronomy and is then taken up by Jesus as he faced temptations from the devil (as recorded in Matthew 4:4). Jesus' firm rebuttal of the idea allowed him to point out to his tempter, the devil, that life is about much more than physical maintenance. Food isn't the only thing a person needs. There are spiritual needs as well, especially for the words that God speaks.

# Manna from heaven

*And when the dew that lay was gone up, behold, upon the face of the wilderness there lay a small round thing, as*

*small as the hoar frost on the ground. And when the*
*children of Israel saw it, they said one to another, It is*
*manna: for they wist not what it was. And Moses said unto*
*them, This is the bread which the LORD hath given you*
*to eat.*

**Exodus 16:14–15**

Someone who, having fallen upon hard times, buys a
lottery ticket and wins the jackpot, might look upon
his or her good fortune as *manna from heaven*. It represents a fantastic stroke of luck, coming just at the right
time. Manna came just at the right time for the Israelites
too. Hungry and disillusioned from their journey in
the desert, they woke up one morning to discover the
ground was carpeted with an edible foodstuff. They
didn't recognise it and asked each other what it was. The
Hebrew for their question was *manna* (literally 'What
is it?'), and it is from this that the foodstuff derives its
name.

## Many are called but few are chosen

*And when the king came in to see the guests, he saw there*
*a man which had not on a wedding garment. Then said the*
*king to the servants, Bind him hand and foot, and take him*
*away, and cast him into outer darkness; there shall be*

*weeping and gnashing of teeth. For many are called, but few are chosen.*

Matthew 22:11, 13–14

When we remark that *many are called, but few are chosen* we mean that entry into a particular group is harder than it would appear to be. There may be many people who seem to have the necessary requirements or qualifications, but that does not mean they can all join; on the contrary – in reality only a few will be able to do so. The expression appears in Matthew's Gospel, at the conclusion of a parable of Jesus. A king had invited a great many people to his son's wedding reception, but when many refused to come, he sent his servants into the highways and byways to invite whoever they came across. One of these last-minute guests was dressed inappropriately, and therefore excluded from the festivities by the king. Jesus concluded his tale with these salutary words, advising his followers to take nothing for granted.

# The mark of Cain

*See* The **curse of Cain**

# Matrix

*That thou shalt set apart unto the LORD all that openeth*
*the matrix, and every firstling that cometh of a beast*
*which thou hast; the males shall be the LORD's.*

**Exodus 13:12**

You might be forgiven for thinking of Neo and men in
dark glasses when you hear the word *matrix*, but the
Bible's use of the word here predates the well-known
film by millennia. Alternatively, you could understand
the word to mean a rectangular array of elements (or
entries) set out by rows and columns. A less used sense
is that of an enclosure from which something might orig-
inate or develop. This latter concept derives from the
Latin for *womb* and is the one which is used in Exodus
13:12 where the verse talks of the first creature to open
a womb: in other words, the first-born.

# Maundy Thursday

*A new commandment I give unto you, That ye love one*
*another; as I have loved you, that ye also love one another.*
*By this shall all men know that ye are my disciples, if ye*
*have love one to another.*

**John 13:34–35**

*Maundy Thursday* is the name given to the Thursday before Easter, which commemorates Christ's Last Supper with his disciples. The name comes from the Old French word *mandé*, meaning 'commanded'; this word in turn comes from the Latin *mandatum*, or 'commandment', which occurs in the Latin translation of Christ's words in John 13:34, *Mandatum novum do vobis* – 'A new commandment I give unto you.' This new commandment was 'that ye love one another as I have loved you', and had been shown by Jesus' washing of his disciples' feet.

Tradition has it that on *Maundy Thursday* the reigning British monarch presents specially minted money to a number of elderly people (one man and one woman for each year of his or her life) in a chosen cathedral city. Originally, the monarch washed the feet of a few poor people and then distributed food and clothes, but the former custom fell into abeyance and the latter was replaced by the giving of money.

# Methuselah

*See* **Jeroboam; As old as Methuselah**

## A millstone around someone's neck

*But whoso shall offend one of these little ones which believe in me, it were better for him that a millstone were hanged about his neck, and that he were drowned in the depth of the sea.*

**Matthew 18:6**

If you are struggling under the weight of some great burden or apparently insurmountable difficulty, you might be said to *have a millstone around your neck*. In biblical times the millstone was the uppermost of two heavy stones used for grinding corn. If it were tied around your neck and you were subsequently thrown into water, drowning would be inevitable. It may seem remarkable that Jesus, of all people, should talk of such an object being used for the purpose of terminating a life, but it highlights his strong feelings towards anyone who deliberately leads another person, especially a child, astray.


## Moderation

*Let your moderation be known unto all men. The Lord is at hand.*

**Philippians 4:5**

*Moderation* is widely understood today to mean taking a sensible attitude towards life. It can apply to a wide range of situations but is most frequently used in relation to bodily intake. If you drink and eat in moderation it means you do not go to great excesses of consumption. In Philippians, Paul is not encouraging people to cut back in this way (although he may do so in other places in the New Testament). The word *moderation* here means to be gentle, kind and patient.

## Money is the root of all evil

*See* The **love of money is the root of all evil**

## A Moses basket

*And when she could not longer hide him, she took for him an ark of bulrushes, and daubed it with slime and with pitch, and put the child therein; and she laid it in the flags by the river's brink.*

**Exodus 2:3**

Despite today's world of synthetic materials it is again becoming popular to put a young baby to sleep in a portable wickerwork cot. Such an item is also known as a *Moses basket*, named after the vessel Moses' mother made for him out of papyrus reeds. She placed him in this waterproof cradle and set it afloat on the River Nile. Her motivation for doing this was, perhaps surprisingly (what would Social Services say of such apparent neglect today?) that she was trying to protect her son from Pharaoh's edict that every male child should be drowned in the Nile. It was the desperate act of a desperate mother.

## Most Holy Place

*See* **Holy of holies**

# N

## Naughtiness; naughty

*Wherefore lay apart all filthiness and superfluity of naughtiness, and receive with meekness the engrafted word, which is able to save your souls.*

**James 1:21**

When we think of the word *naughty* we immediately think of a child who has been caught in some act of misbehaviour, such as raiding the biscuit tin, refusing to go to bed on time or colouring the wallpaper in a range of fluorescent and (usually) permanent scribbles. The definition can stretch to the adult world where we are prone to indulge in something that we probably should avoid, such as cream cakes or shoe shops. In the seventeenth century, the word had a far stronger connotation – that of unabated wickedness. It is this less playful meaning that the translators of the King James Version had in mind when translating Paul's language in James 1:21.

# Nebuchadnezzar

*See* **Jeroboam**

# Nephew

*And he had forty sons and thirty nephews, that rode on threescore and ten ass colts: and he judged Israel eight years.*

Judges 12:14

*He shall neither have son nor nephew among his people, nor any remaining in his dwellings.*

Job 18:19

In modern Western culture the term *nephew* is exclusively applied to any male child of your brother or sister. Greater exposure to other cultures has expanded the meaning of the word, and to some extent reintroduced the meaning that was common at the time the King James Version was written. Then the word could have two meanings: grandson, or descendant in general. In the quotation from Judges we read that Abdon had 'forty sons and thirty nephews' which meant that he had forty sons and thirty grandsons. The Hebrew word from which it was translated actually means 'sons of sons'. Elsewhere, such as in the example from Job, 'descendant' is meant.

Here the verse is saying that the wicked person will have no descendants and therefore be unable to leave anything to posterity.

## New Jerusalem

*And I John saw the holy city, new Jerusalem, coming down from God out of heaven, prepared as a bride adorned for her husband.*

**Revelation 21:2**

The *New Jerusalem* is, quite simply, heaven. It was this city that the apostle John glimpsed in his revelation. The expression has been used by many people to express the future hope of paradise. Blake wrote (and England's rugby supporters sing) of constructing the new Jerusalem in England's green and pleasant land. Others who have taken up this theme include the rock group, Genesis.

## New wine in old bottles

*Neither do men put new wine into old bottles: else the bottles break, and the wine runneth out, and the bottles perish: but they put new wine into new bottles, and both are preserved.*

**Matthew 9:17**

The danger of putting new wine into old bottles is perhaps less evident today when containers are made of inflexible glass. When Jesus uttered the phrase, wine bottles, or wine skins as some modern translations record, were made of animal skins. When new, if still-fermenting wine was placed in them, they were able to expand in line with the reactions taking place inside the liquid. When old, they were rigid and unable to cope in the same way they had been able when new. To put new wine into an old skin was therefore a recipe for disaster which would undoubtedly result in the destruction of the skin and loss of the wine. New wine must be put into fresh, adaptable skins.

## No peace for the wicked

*There is no peace, saith my God, to the wicked.*

**Isaiah 57:21**

The most likely context in which we hear the words *there's no peace for the wicked* is when someone is feeling under pressure. The comment is usually wry or humorous and there is rarely any real moral dimension to it. In the original context in the book of Isaiah, the wicked are compared to the continually heaving seas that are never still for one moment. Like the oceans they can never truly be at peace.

# No respecter of persons

*Then Peter opened his mouth, and said, Of a truth I
perceive that God is no respecter of persons.*

**Acts 10:34**

According to Acts 10:34, God is no respecter of persons.
In today's climate such words might give the idea that
he doesn't think much of people. Such a notion does
not sit very easily with the rest of the Bible, however.
Originally the English word *person* was strongly associated with the Latin word *persona*, which carried with it
the concept of a mask. It concentrated on the individual's
outer, visible trappings such as clothing, bearing and
rank in society, and paid little attention to any internal
qualities or demeanour. The original meaning of the
Greek that the English attempts to encapsulate is that
God doesn't base his judgements on external appear-
ances. Peter had discovered that it didn't matter to God
whether people were Jews or non-Jews. He is less interested in the outside than he is in the inside. Consequently
– and in contrast to us – he doesn't seek to butter up
the rich, glamorous and influential. Bank balances and
the right background or education cut no ice with a God
who, as later translations of this expression clarify, does
not show favouritism.

## No room in the inn

*And she brought forth her firstborn son, and wrapped him in swaddling clothes, and laid him in a manger; because there was no room for them in the inn.*

**Luke 2:7**

Contemporary usage of the expression *no room in the inn* is very similar to the meaning of the original. When Joseph and the expectant Mary arrived in Bethlehem there was no spare accommodation for them in the town. The only place made available to them was the rough-and-ready shelter used for animals. Similarly, anyone using the phrase today means that they can't find any suitable lodgings.

## Noisome

*Surely he shall deliver thee from the snare of the fowler, and from the noisome pestilence.*

**Psalm 91:3**

The word *noisome* is unlikely to be used today, but may conjure up the idea of neighbours from hell or the deep persistent thudding that resonates from a night club in the early hours of the morning. However, it doesn't actually mean 'noisy' but refers to bad smells. It has a more serious meaning here, though – the word *noisome* in the King James Version is translated variously in modern versions of Psalm 91:3: *deadly, perilous* or *fatal*. It was in fact just at the time the King James Version was being developed that the word was undergoing the transition in meaning from 'hurtful' to its present meaning. Interestingly, in 1 Timothy 6:9 the word *noisome* was used in earlier translations than the King James Version, from Tyndale to the Bishops' Bible, but was translated as hurtful in the KJV: 'But they that will be rich fall into temptation and a snare, and into many foolish and hurtful lusts, which drown men in destruction and perdition.'

## Not as other people are

*The Pharisee stood and prayed thus with himself, God, I thank thee, that I am not as other men are, extortioners, unjust, adulterers, or even as this publican.*

**Luke 18:11**

The Pharisees were sticklers for the law, so when the words 'I thank thee that I am not as other men are' come from this man's lips, it's no surprise to see the sort of people he was glad not to be like: extortioners, adulterers and everyone else in between. His attitude was one of confident disdain, coupled with smug self-satisfaction. So to be *not as other people are* means to be aloof, superior and generally better than the riff-raff who have the discourtesy to infest the same world as yourself – with no awareness that they might look at you in the same way.

## Not know what they do

*See* **Know not what they do**

## Not let the sun go down on your anger

*Be ye angry, and sin not: let not the sun go down upon your wrath.*

**Ephesians 4:26**

To *not let the sun go down on your anger* means not to harbour annoyance and resentment: it ought to be dealt with before going to sleep so that we do not carry it through to the next day. Otherwise it will fester and infect both thoughts and attitudes to an ever-increasing extent. In Paul's instructions regarding the way he expected Christians to deal with this emotion, he likened the failure to deal with anger as tantamount to allowing the devil to gain a foothold in their community.

# Not to suffer fools gladly

*For ye suffer fools gladly, seeing ye yourselves are wise.*

**2 Corinthians 11:19**

We've all come across people who *don't suffer fools gladly*. They are not tolerant of the failings of others and they are usually very good at making their opinions known to all and sundry. The Christians in Corinth to whom Paul wrote were the exact opposite of this. He accused them of being far too indulgent and tolerant of people whom he thought they should have avoided completely. By associating with such people, the Corinthians, priding themselves on their wisdom and insight, showed themselves to be anything but wise.

# Nothing new under the sun

*The thing that hath been, it is that which shall be; and that which is done is that which shall be done: and there is no new thing under the sun.*

**Ecclesiastes 1:9**

Reading the tabloid newspapers or the Bible forces the admission that there is *nothing new under the sun*. Whether it's King David or a soap star caught in a compromising situation, there really is nothing that hasn't been said, thought or done in the past. Whether used to describe a negative situation or a positive one, this phrase tends to carry a sense of weary cynicism. You can almost hear the older, wiser head – just like Solomon, the writer of Ecclesiastes, whose goal in life it was to gain wisdom and understanding – dispensing advice to an enthusiastic youngster horrified at the latest dire revelation of inhumanity, or convinced that the wheel has just been invented.

# O

## O ye of little faith

*And he saith unto them, Why are ye fearful, O ye of little faith? Then he arose, and rebuked the winds and the sea; and there was a great calm.*

**Matthew 8:26**

Pulling off some amazing feat under the full glare of those who have doubted our ability, we might conclude our performance with a smug look and a flippant rebuke, 'O ye of little faith.' The words, when originally uttered by Jesus, were part of a more severe rebuke to his disciples who on the particular occasion cited in Matthew were afraid of a storm, even though Jesus was present and, as he swiftly proved, had the capacity to bring the storm to an abrupt end.

## As old as Methuselah

*And all the days of Methuselah were nine hundred sixty and nine years: and he died.*

**Genesis 5:27**

The rather disconcerting lot of any parent is that their children invariably consider them to be as old as Methuselah. What they mean by this is that their mother or father is really ancient, possibly prehistoric and definitely *so yesterday*. The Bible records that Methuselah, one of the early patriarchs who flit ácross the pages of Genesis, lived to the ripe old age of 969 years. A close inspection of what we are told of the man's life reveals only that he died in the same year that the great flood destroyed all the world except for his grandson Noah and his family. Could it be that having already lived longer than anyone else on earth, Methuselah perished only because of the flood?

*See also* **Jeroboam**

## An olive branch

*And he stayed yet other seven days; and again he sent forth the dove out of the ark; and the dove came in to him in the evening; and, lo, in her mouth was an olive leaf*

*pluckt off: so Noah knew that the waters were abated*
*from off the earth.*

**Genesis 8:10–11**

An *olive branch* is a widely recognised symbol of peace.
If a country, army or individual person offers an olive
branch they are reaching out in peace to their enemies.
Given the symbolism of the olive branch it is curious that
the biblical account does not carry this sense, although
it is does mark a breakthrough in the fortunes of life
on earth. There are no warring factions, and the olive
branch is not offered by one group, rather brought back
by a bird in its beak. It may be, therefore, that the imagery
owes more to Greek and Roman cultures than an ancient
Jewish one.

## Out of the mouths of babes

*Out of the mouth of babes and sucklings hast thou*
*ordained strength because of thine enemies, that thou*
*mightest still the enemy and the avenger.*

**Psalm 8:2**

When parents hear their child make some insightful
remark, or perhaps express an opinion about a guest that
they themselves would not have dared utter, he or she

might laughingly be heard to say, *Out of the mouths of babes and infants...* What is meant is that a child, in his or her naivety, innocence, and possibly ignorance of social mores, has said something that older and supposedly wiser people have failed to observe – or have been too diplomatic to say themselves. The phrase appears in Psalm 8 where its inclusion highlights God's use of these apparently insignificant members of the human race to shame those who ought to know better.

## Outer darkness

*But the children of the kingdom shall be cast out into outer darkness: there shall be weeping and gnashing of teeth.*

Matthew 8:12

*Then said the king to the servants, Bind him hand and foot, and take him away, and cast him into outer darkness; there shall be weeping and gnashing of teeth.*

Matthew 22:13

*And cast ye the unprofitable servant into outer darkness: there shall be weeping and gnashing of teeth.*

Matthew 25:30

People who talk of *outer darkness* are usually referring to some fearful place of exclusion rather than somewhere that literally is without light, showing that our modern usage is firmly built on these biblical uses of the phrase. Jesus speaks of outer darkness on three occasions in Matthew's Gospel in the New Testament. He uses it to refer to the place of God's final judgement on individuals.

# P

## Palsy

*And his fame went throughout all Syria: and they brought unto him all sick people that were taken with divers diseases and torments, and those which were possessed with devils, and those which were lunatick, and those that had the palsy; and he healed them.*

Matthew 4:24

The most commonly recognised use of the word *palsy* today comes in its association with cerebral palsy. This is a general term used by doctors to refer to a range of neurological conditions affecting movement and co-ordination. In the sixteenth century *palsy* was used commonly to describe any form of paralysis. Thus, in Matthew the term is used to describe people who were paralysed. Interestingly, some have argued that due to the frequency with which this disease appears in connection with Jesus' healing ministry, there might have been some form of epidemic, possibly caused by polio during that era.

# Paps

*And in the midst of the seven candlesticks one like unto the Son of man, clothed with a garment down to the foot, and girt about the paps with a golden girdle.*

**Revelation 1:13**

*And it came to pass, as he spake these things, a certain woman of the company lifted up her voice, and said unto him, Blessed is the womb that bare thee, and the paps which thou hast sucked.*

**Luke 11:27**

*Paps* is an archaic word meaning 'breasts'. It was used to describe both male and female organs. There are two possible origin for this word, one the Latin *papilla* meaning 'nipple' and the other *pappare*, 'to eat'.

# Pass all understanding

*And the peace of God, which passeth all understanding, shall keep your hearts and minds through Christ Jesus.*

**Philippians 4:7**

Anything which *passes all understanding* is a concept or an idea that is very hard to understand. We might use the phrase in a critical manner to express our own dismay or disgust: 'What she sees in him *passes all understanding*', or to expose our own limitations: 'Pure maths *passes all understanding* as far as I'm concerned.' In Philippians, the apostle Paul used the expression to describe God's peace – something he believed to be real, but difficult to comprehend.

## Pass by on the other side

*And by chance there came down a certain priest that way: and when he saw him, he passed by on the other side. And likewise a Levite, when he was at the place, came and looked on him, and passed by on the other side.*

Luke 10:31–32

In the parable of the **good Samaritan**, Jesus refers to a priest and a Levite, both respectable, upright Jews – surely the obvious candidates to offer help and assistance to the stricken traveller who had been mugged by robbers. On the contrary, both characters *passed by on the other side*. Neither lifted a finger, preferring to distance themselves from the man and his injuries. So someone who passes by on the other side shows no interest in lending a hand where it is needed and callously goes about their own business, refusing to get involved in helping with the troubles of others.

## The patience of Job

*Behold, we count them happy which endure. Ye have heard of the patience of Job, and have seen the end of the Lord; that the Lord is very pitiful, and of tender mercy.*

James 5:11

Anyone who has *the patience of Job* is very fortunate indeed. Such a person is able to face and endure disaster after disaster with cheery fortitude and determination. This man Job suffered a series of trials and difficulties that included the loss of his family and all his possessions, and a decline into ill health. Yet even through these dreadful experiences he took everything on the chin and refused to buckle. In his New Testament letter, James holds Job up as a worthy example of someone who is able to endure all manner of troubles.

*See also* A **Job's comforter**


## Peace and goodwill towards men

*Glory to God in the highest, and on earth peace, good will toward men.*

Luke 2:14

On the first Christmas Day, an angel appeared to a group of shepherds during their night watch and told them of the birth of Jesus in the nearby town of Bethlehem. Once this news had been related, other angels joined the first angel and together they praised God, declaring, *Peace, good will toward men.* This is why the phrase is often used at Christmas time, partly as a form of blessing and partly as a greeting. The festive season is strongly associated with this idea of peace, and many are inclined to look upon others with a far more benevolent eye than would normally be the case throughout the rest of the year.

## A pearl of great price

*Again, the kingdom of heaven is like unto a merchant man, seeking goodly pearls: who, when he had found one pearl of great price, went and sold all that he had, and bought it.*

Matthew 13:45–46

A *pearl of great price* is something that is highly valuable: so much so as to be worth securing at whatever cost. Jesus used the illustration in a parable to show the preciousness of discovering heaven's kingdom. It is one of a number of pithy parables that he told in order to explain what the kingdom of heaven was like. Using everyday objects and situations, sometimes in an enigmatic manner, his parables carry an incisive and penetrating message for those who hear them.

## Peculiar

*For thou art an holy people unto the LORD thy God, and the LORD hath chosen thee to be a peculiar people unto himself, above all the nations that are upon the earth.*

**Deuteronomy 14:2**

When we talk of someone being *peculiar*, we usually mean that they are odd. It is certainly not used in a complimentary tone of voice and often hides a stronger sense of disgust, horror or amazement. Nevertheless, the word appears in the King James Version in a setting which would lead anyone to suspect that it had a completely different meaning from today's. In the quotation above, surely it is unlikely that the writer intended to imply that God had chosen the Israelites to be odd? In fact, in the past, *peculiar* had a possessive sense and signified simply that which belonged to somebody. Thus, the meaning of the verse is that God had chosen the people to be his very own. In addition there is also a hint of special value, which more recent translations have acknowledged by the use of the phrase 'treasured possession'.

## Physician, heal yourself

*And he said unto them, Ye will surely say unto me this proverb, Physician, heal thyself: whatsoever we have heard done in Capernaum, do also here in thy country.*

Luke 4:23

When we say, *Physician, heal thyself*, we are telling someone to apply to themselves the same set of standards, advice and assistance that they give out to others. Or we might ask them to 'take some of their own medicine'. The phrase is no longer addressed to the medical profession – but can apply to all walks of life. Jesus said these words when he returned to his home town of Nazareth, but the phrase was clearly common parlance even then. He had caused something of a stir throughout the region and the crowds turned out in force to see if he would do and say some of the things they had heard about – but he refused, and eventually left, though only after a threatening confrontation.

# Play the fool

*Then said Saul, I have sinned: return, my son David: for I will no more do thee harm, because my soul was precious in thine eyes this day: behold, I have played the fool, and have erred exceedingly.*

1 Samuel 26:21

There may be only one thing to be said to someone who *plays the fool*: 'Stop!' In some situations playing the fool can be harmless fun and amusing for anyone watching; in others the foolishness may have gone beyond such a point. Our use of the term may hark back more to the idea of the medieval court jester than the kind of foolish behaviour Saul refers to, but nonetheless, for best results, the advice is: it is best not to continue to act so foolishly.

# The poor are always with us

*Why was not this ointment sold for three hundred pence, and given to the poor? This he said, not that he cared for the poor; but because he was a thief, and had the bag, and bare what was put therein. Then said Jesus, Let her alone: against the day of my burying hath she kept this. For the poor always ye have with you; but me ye have not always.*

John 12:5–8

Successive announcements, statements and policy promises from those who govern us merely seem to confirm what John recorded from the lips of Jesus in John's Gospel. *The poor are always with us.* This is not meant in a fatalistic way, and should by no means prevent us trying to alleviate the sufferings of the poor – but in this instance, Jesus' point is that that there would always be opportunities to help poor people, because they would always be there, whereas he would not.

## The powers that be

*Let every soul be subject unto the higher powers. For there is no power but of God: the powers that be are ordained of God.*

**Romans 13:1**

*The powers that be* are the rulers or governments of the day, indeed all those in positions of authority and who therefore have the power to make and implement decisions. Frequently this means central government, but it can also indicate local government or any other body that has jurisdiction over a particular sphere of life. Thus the governing body over a particular sport could be referred to in this manner, with reference to a slightly vague body or grouping that can be collectively dismissed in this way. Often, though not always, the phrase is used with a negative connotation. 'The powers that be aren't willing to do anything about it.' When Paul spoke of the powers that be he was specifically referring to temporal rulers and governments, all of which he believed were ultimately given their authority by God.

## Pride goes before a fall

*Pride goeth before destruction, and an haughty spirit before a fall.*

**Proverbs 16:18**

If someone self-confident comes unstuck, having previously asserted that all is well, we quickly shake our heads and mutter under our breaths, *Pride goes before a fall*. What we mean is that those who are overly assured of their position, ability or self-worth very often discover that their self-assurance was misplaced and they weren't in as strong a position as they believed themselves to be. The saying is an abridged version of a verse in Proverbs – a collection of apposite wisdom phrases that were very much a part of the culture of the ancient Near East.

# The prodigal son

Luke 15:11–32

The expression *prodigal son* does not actually appear in the Bible text, but has become the accepted name for this parable and for one of the main characters in this story Jesus told of two brothers, the younger of whom unwisely squanders his share of their father's inheritance. The word *prodigal* actually means wasteful, but largely because of this story – where the son's journeys away from home and then back to it are so critical – people commonly think of it as describing a wanderer. Thus if a friend has been absent for a long period of time, and then returns to take up once more the threads he or she had left, we may hail them as the returning prodigal. There may be some measure of censure in acknowledging them, an attitude which reflects that of the elder brother in Jesus' parable.

*See also* **Kill the fatted calf**

# The promised land

*And Abram took Sarai his wife, and Lot his brother's son, and all their substance that they had gathered, and the souls that they had gotten in Haran; and they went forth to go into the land of Canaan; and into the land of Canaan they came. And Abram passed through the land unto the place of Sichem, unto the plain of Moreh. And the Canaanite was then in the land. And the LORD appeared unto Abram, and said, Unto thy seed will I give this land: and there builded he an altar unto the LORD, who appeared unto him. And he removed from thence unto a mountain on the east of Beth-el, and pitched his tent, having Beth-el on the west, and Ha-i on the east: and there he builded an altar unto the LORD, and called upon the name of the LORD.*

**Genesis 12:5–8**

To the Jews of the Old Testament, the Promised Land was the strictly geographical area known as Canaan. This was the place God had promised to Abraham, the father of the nation. Abraham himself did not actually own any of the land, but it eventually came into the possession of his descendants after they had escaped from Egypt under Moses' leadership. Today, whilst the expression still retains its geographical sense (either specific to Israel or with reference to some other cherished location), it can also refer to any situation that represents the ultimate realisation of a person's dreams or hopes. So we can say, 'When he was promoted to Chief Executive he felt as if he had arrived in *the promised land*.'

*See also* A **land flowing with milk and honey**

# A prophet is without honour in his own country

*And he said, Verily I say unto you, No prophet is accepted in his own country.*

Luke 4:24

If a friend or relative of ours achieves a measure of fame or celebrity, we may respond in two ways. One would be to bask in their glory and emphasise our ties to them. The other would be to denigrate their new position and regale all and sundry with uncomplimentary tales about the real person that we know. It is this latter possibility that Jesus highlighted when speaking to his hostile compatriots in Nazareth. He criticised them because everywhere else people were more than happy to receive him. But back home, among his own people, with those who knew him and his family, he was given a cold reception.

# Publican

*And, behold, there was a man named Zacchaeus, which was the chief among the publicans, and he was rich.*

Luke 19:2

When we think of a publican we think of the (possibly mythical) jolly character who owns and runs the Rose and Crown or the Boar's Head in the High Street. To read such a quintessentially British occupation back into the world of the Ancient Near East would cause us to misunderstand what the word *publican* refers to when it appears in the pages of the King James Version. The most famous publican in the Bible is probably Zacchaeus, a short man who wished to see Jesus. He was a tax collector by profession, earning his living taking money from citizens and placing it in the public purse of the Roman state (with plenty of freedom to divert substantial amounts into his own private funds). His collusion with the foreign invading power and the inevitable contact such a position necessitated with Gentiles gained him, and all those who performed the same function, universal disapproval from his fellow Jews.

# Q

## The quick and the dead

*And he commanded us to preach unto the people, and to testify that it is he which was ordained of God to be the Judge of quick and dead.*

**Acts 10:42**

If we call someone *quick*, we either mean they are physically able to move themselves swiftly from one place to another, or that their mind is able to assimilate new information rapidly. (Or the word may be used in the negative to make fun of someone who is, by contrast, slow.) Whether they are nimble of brain or of foot, at least they share something in common with the archaic use of the word, when *quick* meant 'alive' and was often used in contrast — as in the above example from Acts — to death. Here Peter announces to his listeners that Jesus has been appointed by God to be the judge of both the living and the dead.

# R

## The rain falls on the just and the unjust

*That ye may be the children of your Father which is in heaven: for he maketh his sun to rise on the evil and on the good, and sendeth rain on the just and on the unjust.*

**Matthew 5:45**

When we say that *the rain falls on the just and the unjust* we mean that pleasant things happen to both good and bad people. We might wish to live in a world where good people are rewarded and bad people are punished, but life isn't as simple as that. In the Sermon on the Mount, Jesus pointed out to his listeners that God was indiscriminate in distributing his acts of kindness universally, irrespective of the kind of people who would benefit – whether they were worthy to receive them or not. He did this to encourage people to be similarly benevolent in their behaviour towards others.

# Raise Cain

Genesis 4:3–12

If you are the sort of person who *raises Cain*, it is quite likely that the police will be interested in your activities. It refers to a violent troublemaker. The expression derives from the first murderer in the Bible, Cain, who killed his brother out of jealousy. The word *raise* in this context carries the idea of conjuring up, much as a person might summon an evil spirit. Consequently, the picture given is that of bringing up the spirit of Cain that was bent upon the destruction of his brother.

# Reap where you have not sown

*Then he which had received the one talent came and said, Lord, I knew thee that thou art an hard man, reaping where thou hast not sown, and gathering where thou hast not strawed.*

Matthew 25:24

Usually the person who *reaps where he* (or *she*) *has not sown* is regarded as lucky: they have gained some benefit from a situation where they have not had any input. We could use it the other way round – when someone has had bad luck despite not having done anything to merit it – but we don't tend to do so. When we say to someone *You reap what you sow*, on the other hand, we are clearly implying that all the bad that's come to them is their own fault. The connection between what is sown and what is reaped occurs several times in the Bible but the only time where reaping what has not been sown comes up is in a parable Jesus told of three servants each given some money by their master. The first two used their money well and earned more from it; they were commended by Jesus. The third one, however, did nothing with his money. In fact, he just hid it in the ground. When his master called him to account, he accused his boss of being an awkward person to work for, making impossible demands upon his employees, cheating people – reaping where he had not sown. The master then punished this third servant.

*See* **Whatever a man sows, that shall he reap**

# Rehoboam

*See* **Jeroboam**

# Render to Caesar

*And he said unto them, Render therefore unto Caesar the things which be Caesar's, and unto God the things which be God's.*

Luke 20:25

Those of us who pay taxes are *rendering to Caesar* the things that belong to him. In other words, we are giving to the authorities what we are expected to give. The phrase means to hand over to any appropriate body those things which we are rightly required to give to them. Whilst the context in which Jesus used the phrase was directly related to an issue of whether the Jews should pay taxes to the conquering and despised Romans, today it is used more widely than in a financial sense. It can refer to any situation where there is a sense of appropriate obligation towards an organisation.

# The road to Damascus

*See* A **Damascus-road experience**

# S

## Sackcloth and ashes

*Woe unto thee, Chorazin! woe unto thee, Bethsaida! for if the mighty works, which were done in you, had been done in Tyre and Sidon, they would have repented long ago in sackcloth and ashes.*

**Matthew 11:21**

In biblical times, wearing an item of coarsely woven material and sprinkling ash over the body showed the world that someone was passing through a period of mourning or repentance. The rough garment and the use of the dry dust were visible signs of inward grief and sorrow over what had happened. The physical discomfort they caused mirrored the spiritual discomfort felt inside the person. Jesus used this expression when he denounced some of the towns he had visited, saying that if notoriously wicked places such as Tyre and Sidon had had the opportunity of hearing what they had heard, they would have immediately reacted by turning away from their sins with expressions of true sadness.

# Salmanazar

*See* **Jeroboam**

# The salt of the earth

*Ye are the salt of the earth: but if the salt have lost his savour, wherewith shall it be salted? it is thenceforth good for nothing, but to be cast out, and to be trodden under foot of men.*

Matthew 5:13

If you've ever slapped someone on the back and described him or her as *the salt of the earth*, you were telling them what a wonderful person they are. A person so described is usually reliable, generous and helpful. In Jesus' day, salt was used not just for seasoning – or gritting roads in winter – but for preserving and cleansing too. He therefore used it to describe the kind of good qualities he expected in those who were listening to him as he gave his Sermon on the Mount.

# Say the word

*The centurion answered and said, Lord, I am not worthy that thou shouldest come under my roof: but speak the word only, and my servant shall be healed.*

Matthew 8:8

In Matthew's Gospel, the man who said *speak the word*, from which this phrase derives, showed that he had an absolute trust in Jesus' ability to heal his sick servant, even without actually needing to go and see him. So this phrase has become a promise to carry out an allotted task immediately upon instruction: 'Just say the word and I'll do it.'

# Scales fell from my eyes

*And immediately there fell from his eyes as it had been scales: and he received sight forthwith, and arose, and was baptized.*

Acts 9:18

The apostle Paul had been blinded by a bright light as he was making his way towards Damascus (see A **Damascus-road experience**). After three days without sight he was visited by a man called Ananias, who prayed for him. As he did so, the writer tells us that it was as if scales had been peeled from his eyes and he was able to see. While this was clearly a physical phenomenon, the expression is more often used in a moral or intellectual sense today, building on its connection with the revelation Saul had on the road. When the scales fall from our eyes, it means that we have had some dramatic epiphany, perhaps seeing for the first time how something works, or else either reversing or overturning our previous view of things.

## Scapegoat

*And Aaron shall cast lots upon the two goats; one lot for the LORD, and the other lot for the scapegoat.*

**Leviticus 16:8**

When things go wrong in life it is common for us to look around for someone or something else we can blame for what has taken place – a *scapegoat*. Political parties do it after they fail to win a seat or election; sports teams might do it when they lose an important match; and businesses will do the same when they underperform. The word *scapegoat* comes from Leviticus, where God instructed the priests first to take two goats. Then, by lot, one would be chosen for sacrifice, and the other would be banished into the desert. It was this latter creature that was called the *scapegoat*, Tyndale having coined the word from *escape* and *goat*. The event was rich in symbolism: the sins of the people were paid for through the sacrifice and at the same time removed from their sight for ever.

## See the light

*See* A **Damascus-road experience**

## See through a glass darkly

*See* **Through a glass darkly**

## Seethe

*The first of the firstfruits of thy land thou shalt bring into the house of the LORD thy God. Thou shalt not seethe a kid in his mother's milk.*

**Exodus 23:19**

If somebody is seething with anger, we know that it is best to leave him or her alone until they calm down. Their behaviour brings to mind the picture of a cartoon character with steam coming out of its ears, its face turning red in frustration and rage. In the King James Version the word *seethe* means 'to boil'. Immediately we can see that while it is unlikely that any of us have ever used it when talking of cooking, the fundamental meaning is obvious, and the same now as then. We could quite easily describe the angry person as letting their emotions come to the boil. The Israelites were commanded not to cook or boil a kid – in the sense of a young goat, rather than a child – in the milk of its mother.

## Separate the sheep from the goats
*See* **Divide the sheep from the goats**

## Separate the wheat from the chaff
*Whose fan is in his hand, and he will throughly purge his floor, and gather his wheat into the garner; but he will burn up the chaff with unquenchable fire.*

**Matthew 3:12**

When we separate the wheat from the chaff, we are subdividing a group into two subgroups. In one go the valuable, important items, and in the other those that are of little use and can be discarded. In farming, this process was performed by tossing all the items into the air and allowing the wind to differentiate the heavier grains of wheat from the lighter chaff, the worthless husk of the cereal which would be blown away. Alternatively, it could be done artificially by an individual creating a current of air, as is described in Matthew. Here a metaphorical fan is placed in the hands of Jesus who carries out the process of judging between the good and the bad.

## Sermon on the Mount

Expressions that derive from the words of Jesus' *Sermon on the Mount* include: **The beam in your eye; Cast pearls before swine; Consider the lilies; Our daily bread; An eye for an eye; The golden rule; Hide your light under a bushel; In all his (or her) glory; A jot or tittle; Judge not that ye be not judged; Know them by their fruits; Your left hand does not know what your right hand is doing; The rain falls on the just and the unjust; The salt of the earth; Serve God and Mammon; The straight and narrow; Turn the other cheek; A wolf in sheep's clothing**.

## Serve God and Mammon/serve two masters

*No man can serve two masters: for either he will hate the one, and love the other; or else he will hold to the one, and despise the other. Ye cannot serve God and mammon.*

Matthew 6:24

The thrust of both of these expressions is that it is impossible to maintain two contradictory commitments in life. For example, you simply can't support both Liverpool and Everton, or Arsenal and Tottenham Hotspur. It is out of the question. Sooner or later, probably sooner, something will have to give. Jesus was highlighting the impossibility of being devoted to money and being devoted to God. The origins of the word *mammon* lie in the Aramaic word for *riches*. This foreign word was incorporated into English versions because translators believed that coveting and chasing after money were forms of idolatry, behind which lurked a specific malign influence, Mammon.

## Several

*And the LORD smote the king, so that he was a leper unto*

*the day of his death, and dwelt in a several house. And Jotham the king's son was over the house, judging the people of the land.*

**2 Kings 15:5**

We use the word *several* to mean simply 'a few'. In answer to the question, 'How many times have you watched that film?' our reply might be, 'I don't know precisely — but several times'. The verse in 2 Kings 15:5 reads awkwardly in English. *A several house* does not make sense from a grammatical perspective, so it clearly had a different meaning from the one we are accustomed to today. In this context *several* meant 'separate'. According to Jewish law, lepers had to live in isolation from others. Azariah (or Uzziah), the monarch mentioned in this passage, would have been isolated from society, even though he was king, for fear of others contracting the disease. Thus he lived in quarantine, while his son effectively became the ruler.

## Shambles

*Whatsoever is sold in the shambles, that eat, asking no question for conscience sake.*

**1 Corinthians 10:25**

My teacher was surely justified in describing some of my maths homework as a child as a shambles! It was a chaotic meandering of random guesses, more inspired by a misplaced confidence in luck than scientific method. In earlier times, when linguists did not have access to my schoolbooks, the word *shambles* meant a place where meat was sold, and subsequently a slaughterhouse. Paul, in the passage cited in 1 Corinthians, was explaining to his readers – some of whom were concerned that they might be eating food that had been prepared by or for pagan rituals – not to ask questions about its origins. Instead they ought to go ahead and enjoy eating with a clear conscience.

## Shibboleth

*Then Jephthah gathered together all the men of Gilead, and fought with Ephraim: and the men of Gilead smote Ephraim, because they said, Ye Gileadites are fugitives of Ephraim among the Ephraimites, and among the Manassites. And the Gileadites took the passages of Jordan before the Ephraimites: and it was so, that when those Ephraimites which were escaped said, Let me go over; that the men of Gilead said unto him, Art thou an Ephraimite? If he said, Nay; then said they unto him, Say now Shibboleth: and he said Sibboleth: for he could not frame to pronounce*

*it right. Then they took him, and slew him at the passages
of Jordan: and there fell at that time of the Ephraimites
forty and two thousand.*

Judges 12:4–6

A *shibboleth* is a custom, phrase or use of language that
acts as a test or password to see whether someone belongs
to a nation, class or profession. Many people whose
mother tongue is not English have trouble pronouncing
the *th-* sound, and this can make it quite easy to distinguish foreigners. The word *shibboleth* comes from
Judges 12. After a battle between Gilead and Ephraim,
the soldiers from Gilead took up positions by river fords.
When the men of Ephraim tried to cross, they would
claim to be Gileadites. In order to test their credentials
they were asked to say the word *shibboleth*. If they could
only pronounce it as *sibboleth*, their cover would be
exposed and they were killed on the spot.

# The signs of the times

*And in the morning, It will be foul weather today: for the
sky is red and lowring. O ye hypocrites, ye can discern the
face of the sky; but can ye not discern the signs of the times?*

**Matthew 16:3**

Each generation refers regretfully to phenomena that it

recognises to be *signs of the times* – events, particularly unfortunate ones, that are in some way typical of a particular period. They are taken to be proof of moral or other types of decline. 'The fact that leaders never have the honour to resign is just another sign of the times', or 'Children listen more to their friends than their parents – it's a sign of the times.' Jesus criticised those around him who were always asking for proof of his identity, by replying that, just as they were perfectly capable of reading meteorological phenomena, they should have been able to tell who he was by the signs they saw around them.

## Simony

Acts 8:9–24

The term *simony* comes from the name of a converted magician called Simon. It describes the custom of buying and selling spiritual or ecclesiastical benefits or offices. In the book of Acts Simon sees the apostles imparting the Holy Spirit through the laying on of hands, and he then seeks to purchase the ability to do the same. He is told in no uncertain manner that such a precious gift is not one that can be bought with money. This rebuke was swiftly followed by a statement of penitence from Simon.

# Simple

*For your obedience is come abroad unto all men. I am glad therefore on your behalf: but yet I would have you wise unto that which is good, and simple concerning evil.*

**Romans 16:19**

Today we can use the word *simple* to signify a variety of things. Most of these meanings have at their core the idea of something being without complications. If we find a concept simple to understand, it is not very hard to work out. If a new skill is simple to acquire it is easy to learn how to do it. If we call another human being simple we are referring to the fact that they are probably not exceptionally bright – and presumably we hope that the geniuses of this world don't use the same expression of us. In the King James Version the word has a different slant on the same sense. It means that someone or something is transparent, honest, straightforward and without any sense of duplicity. This is how Paul wanted the readers of his letter to the Romans to be.

# Your sin will find you out

*But if ye will not do so, behold, ye have sinned against the LORD: and be sure your sin will find you out.*

**Numbers 32:23**

If details of a person's secret — and quite possibly bad — behaviour come to light, we may say, 'Your sin has found you out'. The phrase means that it is inevitable that sooner or later those involved in wicked activity will be caught out and their actions brought into the light. In Numbers, Moses told the downhearted Israelites that they were to have the courage to occupy the Promised Land, but if they failed to do this then their failure (or sin) would become apparent, and they would suffer its consequences.

## Sincere

*As newborn babes, desire the sincere milk of the word, that ye may grow thereby.*

1 Peter 2:2

To our current way of thinking it is difficult to imagine how milk could possibly be *sincere*. Today we think of the word as meaning 'without deceit' or 'genuine', but this isn't far from its past meaning of 'pure' or 'unadulterated', and it is in this sense that that it was used in the King James Version. Peter addresses his readers, challenging them to hanker after the pure nourishing milk of the word, rather than to accept watered-down, skimmed or low-fat versions.

## Singular

*Speak unto the children of Israel, and say unto them, When a man shall make a singular vow, the persons shall be for the Lord by thy estimation.*

**Leviticus 27:2**

*Singular* today means the opposite of *plural*. It is used to describe something that is on its own – or occasionally it can be used to describe an unusual or strange person or item. Chapter 27 of Leviticus deals with the price to be paid upon making vows to God. When verse 2 speaks of a singular vow, it refers not so much to one vow on its own, but to its being an especially important or significant vow.

## Skin of my teeth

*My bone cleaveth to my skin and to my flesh, and I am escaped with the skin of my teeth.*

**Job 19:20**

Tooth enamel is the hardest substance in our bodies. That makes it good for biting. Skin is one of the softest parts of our bodies. That makes it good for grazing, cutting and peeling. If we had skin on our teeth, meals would be drawn out, chewy affairs – but we don't. When the writer of Job talks about the skin of his teeth, he means avoiding something by an incredibly small, perhaps imperceptible, amount. When we say we have *escaped something by the skin of our teeth*, we mean we have only just managed to steer clear of some disaster or tragedy.

## Sodom and Gomorrah

Genesis 18:16 – 19:29

Sodom and Gomorrah were two cities in the region bordering the Dead Sea and have become synonymous with God's judgement. Throughout the Bible, the behaviour that brought about their destruction is referred to as an example to avoid. God destroyed these cities even though he was forced by Abraham to agree that he would spare them if he was able to find just ten good inhabitants. When fire rained down upon the cities, Abraham's nephew and great-nieces were rescued through the intervention of angels who ushered them to safety.

## Sodomy

Genesis 19:1–11

*Sodomy* is the act of anal intercourse. It may involve two men or a man and a woman. The word is a derivation from the name of the city of Sodom, one of the wicked cities that was destroyed by God in Genesis. The story tells how the town's male inhabitants wanted to have sex with visitors to the house of Lot. It is this aspect of the citizens' behaviour that gave rise to the adaptation of the city's name to describe the act itself. Elsewhere in the Bible other sins of Sodom are highlighted. In Ezekiel 16:49–50 arrogance, greed and a lack of concern for the poor are listed as other sins committed by the people of Sodom.

## A soft answer turns away wrath

*A soft answer turneth away wrath: but grievous words stir up anger.*

**Proverbs 15:1**

Anyone who gets caught up in a potentially violent confrontation will hope to prove the truth of the phrase *a soft answer turns away wrath*. When tempers are flaring and aggression is welling up, it is often best to refuse to rise to the bait, instead responding with a reply that takes the steam and anger out of the situation. The opposite is true, namely that by answering threatening statements with equally heated ones, you are likely to add fuel to an already combustible situation.

## Sow the wind and reap the whirlwind

*For from Israel was it also: the workman made it; therefore it is not God: but the calf of Samaria shall be broken in pieces. For they have sown the wind, and they shall reap the whirlwind: it hath no stalk: the bud shall yield no meal: if so be it yield, the strangers shall swallow it up.*

**Hosea 8:6–7**

Arthur Harris, chief of Britain's bomber command during the Second World War, said of the Germans, *They sowed the wind and now they are going to reap the whirlwind*. What he meant was that, in bombing Britain's town and cities to the extent that they had, they themselves would now be the victims of an immeasurably greater level of sustained attack. This is the principle of *sowing the wind and reaping the whirlwind*. Whatever has been begun by one party – even in an innocent manner – will be visited upon them again with interest, by others. This was what the prophet Hosea predicted for the people of Israel as a consequence of their wicked behaviour towards God.

## Spare the rod and spoil the child

*He that spareth his rod hateth his son: but he that loveth him chasteneth him betimes.*

**Proverbs 13:24**

Reality TV is full of families with children who come across as self-centred, arrogant individuals. The viewer might well be heard to mutter, *Spare the rod and spoil the child*. Today some will use this verse to justify the use of physical punishment, but its interpretation need not be so literal; however, the key is that there should be a way of enforcing behaviour and seeing a youngster face up to the consequences of his or her actions, and thus the spirit of the proverb can be upheld without recourse to corporal punishment.

## The spirit is willing, but the flesh is weak

*Watch and pray, that ye enter not into temptation: the spirit indeed is willing, but the flesh is weak.*

Matthew 26:41

Which of us, when confronted with a tempting display of cakes, has not heard (or at least reflected) that *the spirit is willing but the flesh is weak*? The saying expresses the acceptance that we lack the ability, energy or willpower to put our good intentions into practice. While intellectually or spiritually we might consider doing the right thing, when push comes to shove we find that we are unable to do so. The idea acknowledges the reality that for many of us there can easily be a gulf between what we intend and what actually takes place. Jesus challenged his disciples with these words in the Garden of Geth-semane, the night before his crucifixion. They had expressed their eagerness to be with him, but when he wished to spend time in prayer with them, they were overcome by sleep.

*See also* **Watch and pray**

# The spirit of the law

*See* The **letter of the law**

# Spread your net

*A man that flattereth his neighbour spreadeth a net for his feet.*

**Proverbs 29:5**

In the way we use the term, if you *spread your net*, you are trying to catch or seek a wider range of people or things with a positive aim. In the original biblical context, what is meant is that the person who flatters someone else is laying the groundwork for trapping them into a course of action that is of benefit to the flatterer. An example might be the tried, tested, but perhaps not ultimately successful, 'You are the most generous friend I have', as the precursor to a request for them to prove the worthiness of that accolade by coughing up a financial gift.

## A still small voice

*And after the earthquake a fire; but the LORD was not in the fire: and after the fire a still small voice.*

**1 Kings 19:12**

Sometimes a person will refer to their *still small voice*. What they mean is the gentle tugging of their conscience in difficult moral decision-making. Quiet, but unmistakable, it speaks to them through the hubbub and turmoil, giving them the necessary guidance they need, to do what is right. In the book of 1 Kings, the prophet Elijah experienced a wide (and noisy) range of supernaturally inspired natural phenomena – wind, earthquake and fire. Yet despite their also being of divine origin, it was only when he heard a still small voice that he recognised God actually speaking to him.

# The straight and narrow

*Because strait is the gate, and narrow is the way, which leadeth unto life, and few there be that find it.*

Matthew 7:14

The *straight and narrow* is a path that is considered to be good from a moral perspective. If someone strays from it they usually become the object of self-righteous reproach or, if they are in the limelight, the censure of the tabloid press. Jesus used the expression in the Sermon on the Mount to describe the little-trod pathway to heavenly blessing. He contrasted it with the much-travelled wide or broad road that leads to destruction. The word straight here was originally *strait*, meaning 'narrow' (as in the Straits of Gibraltar), not actually straight: so there is a narrow gate that is therefore hard to find, and a narrow path that is uncomfortable and difficult to follow.

# Strain at a gnat (and swallow a camel)

*Woe unto you, scribes and Pharisees, hypocrites! for ye pay tithe of mint and anise and cummin, and have omitted the weightier matters of the law, judgement, mercy, and faith: these ought ye to have done, and not to leave the other*

*undone. Ye blind guides, which strain at a gnat, and*
*swallow a camel.*

**Matthew 23:23–24**

Theologians have hotly debated the correct wording of
this short phrase. Various theories have been proposed
to arrive at a meaning that makes sense today and does
justice to the expression in its original setting. Some
believe that the right rendering should be 'strain *out* a
gnat' implying that if you spotted an insect in your drink
you would stop drinking until you had extracted it. Similarly, others argue that '*at* a gnat' is correct, with 'strain'
needing a bit more explanation – but arriving at exactly
the same overall meaning. The point of what Jesus was
saying was that some of the religious leaders were so
intent on following the minutiae of the law that they failed
to spot the fact that they were ignoring its more important issues. They may have avoided gulping down a tiny
gnat, but ended up choking on the immeasurably more
important camel.

## A stranger in a strange land

*And she bare him a son, and he called his name Gershom:*
*for he said, I have been a stranger in a strange land.*

**Exodus 2:22**

*A stranger in a strange land* is something of a tautology. By definition a person can only be called a stranger when in an alien setting. I am not a stranger in my own house or country, but am when in the home of someone who doesn't know me or in a land where I don't belong. The point of repeating the *strange* motif is to heighten the sense of alienation or foreignness. *A stranger in a strange land* is definitively isolated and set apart from everything and everyone else that already lives there. In Exodus, Moses calls his son Gershom, which sounded like the Hebrew for 'a foreigner there'. This sense of alienation doubtless had a special poignancy for Moses. Raised in the court of the Pharaoh yet acutely aware of his Israelite roots, he must have been conscious from the beginning that he was caught between different cultures. After his murder of an Egyptian and subsequent flight to a third cultural milieu, this feeling of not really belonging would presumably have been considerably heightened, making its manifestation in the naming of his first child an unsurprising choice.

# Strong meat

*For when for the time ye ought to be teachers, ye have need that one teach you again which be the first principles of the oracles of God; and are become such as have need of milk, and not of strong meat.*

Hebrews 5:12

*Strong meat* is considered to be something that is only suitable for those who are able to cope with it. It need not necessarily refer to food that can (or can't) be eaten — but may be used in the same way that we might describe a lecture or a book as being 'meaty', that is of considerable intellectual weight and a challenge to get to grips with. When the expression was used in the book of Hebrews, the author was complaining that the recipients of the letter were still at the childish stage of requiring milk rather than having progressed to the more adult need for solid meat. He was distressed at this lack of maturity.

# A stumbling block

*Thou shalt not curse the deaf, nor put a stumblingblock before the blind, but shalt fear thy God: I am the LORD.*

**Leviticus 19:14**

*And shall say, Cast ye up, cast ye up, prepare the way, take up the stumblingblock out of the way of my people.*

**Isaiah 57:14**

*Let us not therefore judge one another any more: but judge this rather, that no man put a stumblingblock or an occasion to fall in his brother's way.*

**Romans 14:13**

*But we preach Christ crucified, unto the Jews a stumblingblock, and unto the Greeks foolishness.*

**1 Corinthians 1:23**

The expression a *stumbling block* appears in the Bible in several different passages. Each time it carries the idea of a rock or stone, deliberately and maliciously placed in the way of someone in such a way that the person is likely to trip up, be thrown off balance or upset by its presence. The thrust of the passages is usually that these hindrances should not be placed in front of someone, or if they have been, they should be removed as soon as possible so that no one gets injured. This is certainly the case in the references in Leviticus, Isaiah and Romans. The one from Corinthians is slightly different in that Paul is explaining to the Christians at Corinth that the concept of a crucified Messiah will inevitably be a touchy issue for Jews, but it may not be possible to get them past this contentious point of doctrine. (*See also* 1 Peter 2:8.)

# Subscribe

*And I subscribed the evidence, and sealed it, and took witnesses, and weighed him the money in the balances.*

Jeremiah 32:10

If we *subscribe* to something we usually agree to a particular viewpoint, pay a regular amount of money to receive a magazine or information bulletin or give periodic payments to a charity or organisation in return for membership. In the King James Version the word *subscribe* has a slightly older meaning, namely 'write' or 'sign a document'– literally 'to write underneath'. This is certainly what is conveyed in Jeremiah's account of a legal transaction. Prior to sealing the deed, he *subscribed* it or signed it. This is the origin of our term 'subscription', in that we put our name to the agreement to pay money for said service.

# Suffer fools gladly

*See* **Not to suffer fools gladly**

# Sufficient unto the day is the evil thereof

*Take therefore no thought for the morrow: for the morrow shall take thought for the things of itself. Sufficient unto the day is the evil thereof.*

Matthew 6:34

In a nutshell, the expression *sufficient unto the day is the evil thereof* means that there is enough to worry about today without needing to resort to thinking ahead to the complications and difficulties of tomorrow or subsequent days. It comes from a section of the Sermon on the Mount where Jesus is trying to wean his followers away from the perennial human activity of worrying about what is going to happen in the future. The phrase is often abbreviated as *Sufficient unto the day*.

# T

## Tell

*And he brought him forth abroad, and said, Look now toward heaven, and tell the stars, if thou be able to number them: and he said unto him, So shall thy seed be.*

**Genesis 15:5**

Apart from being the surname of the famed user of the crossbow William Tell, the word *tell* can either be used when we relate something or when we discern something. 'Tell me the time please' has the former sense, while the answer 'I cannot tell what time it is' has the latter. In the King James Version *tell* is used in the sense of knowing, but it is also used to mean 'count' as in this verse from Genesis in which Abraham is challenged to count the number of stars in the sky. This sense is seen in the current usage *teller*, one who counts money, or votes in a ballot.

## Thief in the night

*See* **Like a thief in the night**

## Thirty pieces of silver

*And said unto them, What will ye give me, and I will deliver him unto you? And they covenanted with him for thirty pieces of silver.*

**Matthew 26:15**

When Judas Iscariot discussed with the Jewish author-ities how he might hand his friend Jesus over to them, they agreed to pay him *thirty pieces of silver*. Consequently, the expression is generally used to refer to the price paid for another person's betrayal. Judas never prof-ited directly from this payment since, overcome with remorse at his treachery, he tried to return the coins, then killed himself.

*See also* **Judas**

# A thorn in the flesh/thorn in my side

*And lest I should be exalted above measure through the abundance of the revelations, there was given to me a thorn in the flesh, the messenger of Satan to buffet me, lest I should be exalted above measure.*

**2 Corinthians 12:7**

A *thorn in the flesh* does not refer to the sort of accident that can happen to us when we are smelling roses, picking blackberries or strolling through forest undergrowth. It stands for something that is a constant irritation: what we might call today 'a pain in the neck'. The apostle Paul wrote about his own *thorn in the flesh* without ever explaining what it was. It was clearly a situation that caused him great anguish and he confides to the church at Corinth that he prayed on three specific occasions that this frustrating situation might be taken away from him. It was not, however, removed, but he felt that he was given the power to endure its continuing presence.

## Those who live by the sword will die by the sword

*Then said Jesus unto him, Put up again thy sword into his place: for all they that take the sword shall perish with the sword.*

Matthew 26:52

Jesus spoke these words after one of his disciples had cut off the ear of one of the people who had come to arrest him in the middle of the night. Jesus rebuked him and told him not to behave in this way. Our understanding of what he meant is that anyone who embarks upon a life of death or violence is likely to find that his or her life will end in violence. It would be wrong to suppose that Jesus was guaranteeing that it would happen. Rather, he was merely acknowledging the likelihood of its turning out that way.

## Those whom God has joined together, let no man put asunder

*Wherefore they are no more twain, but one flesh. What therefore God hath joined together, let not man put asunder.*

Matthew 19:6

Anyone who has attended a traditional church marriage ceremony has heard the minister declare, *Those whom God hath joined together, let no man put asunder*. The phrase comes in the *Book of Common Prayer*, but it is derived from Jesus' words recorded by Matthew. He was replying to the Pharisees' questions regarding divorce. In the context of marriage, the statement means that the union of the couple is a divinely ordained institution and, as God himself is the one who has joined one man and one woman, then no human being should attempt to undo this act of God.

## Three score years and ten

*The days of our years are threescore years and ten; and if by reason of strength they be fourscore years, yet is their strength labour and sorrow; for it is soon cut off, and we fly away.*

**Psalm 90:10**

A score is twenty and so it is relatively easy to work out that *three score years and ten* is equivalent to the grand sum of seventy years. This is the average length of time that someone might be expected to live. In the original language the word used is simply 'seventy' rather than that which has been arrived at by an equation, so the expression is a reflection of the English language rather than the Hebrew.

## Through a glass darkly

*For now we see through a glass, darkly; but then face to face: now I know in part; but then shall I know even as also I am known.*

**1 Corinthians 13:12**

To see *through a glass darkly* is not the perspective of a consumer of stout or some such alcoholic beverage. Nor is Paul speaking of an opaque window. 'Glass' here has its more archaic meaning of a mirror, and what he is actually referring to was the kind of highly polished metal that was used in the ancient world as we would use a mirror today. Indeed, more contemporary versions use the word *mirror* rather than *glass*. The phrase can be used to describe the limitations of current knowledge. So a scientist might say, 'As far as quantum physics is concerned, we are merely seeing through a glass darkly', by which he or she would mean that what we do know is sketchy and incomplete. One day, when Jesus Christ returns, we will see the Lord directly and fully.

# A time and a place for everything

*To every thing there is a season, and a time to every purpose under the heaven: a time to be born, and a time to die; a time to plant, and a time to pluck up that which is planted; a time to kill, and a time to heal; a time to break down, and a time to build up;*

*A time to weep, and a time to laugh; a time to mourn, and a time to dance; a time to cast away stones, and a time to gather stones together; a time to embrace, and a time to refrain from embracing; a time to get, and a time to lose; a time to keep, and a time to cast away; a time to rend, and a time to sew; a time to keep silence, and a time to speak; a time to love, and a time to hate; a time of war, and a time of peace.*

**Ecclesiastes 3:1–8**

The expression *a time and a place for everything* has come to mean that, given a specific set of circumstances, any behaviour can be appropriate – although it can also mean the opposite. If someone was behaving in an unnecessarily exuberant manner at a funeral they might be gently reprimanded with these words, *there is a time and place for everything*, but equally someone being excessively sombre at a birthday party might also be reprimanded with the same words. The roots of the expression lie in the observations of the preacher in Ecclesiastes. So it is likely that, rather than suggesting the correctness of actions under particular circumstances, he was merely recording what actually takes place. In other words his viewpoint is 'these things happen,' rather than 'these things ought to happen'.

## To him who has shall more be given

*For unto every one that hath shall be given, and he shall have abundance: but from him that hath not shall be taken away even that which he hath.*

Matthew 25:29

One of the facts of life seems to be that those who already have a great deal invariably obtain even more. In the financial sector, it is those who have money to invest who are able to accumulate more, while those who do not have any in the first place are never able to build up a fund. This is what the phrase *to him who has shall more be given* means. The phrase, which is a slight adaptation of one that appears several times in the Gospels, has come to be used as a salutary warning against squandering or neglecting gifts, abilities and resources.

# To the pure all things are pure

*Unto the pure all things are pure: but unto them that are defiled and unbelieving is nothing pure; but even their mind and conscience is defiled.*

**Titus 1:15**

This phrase gets bandied about to justify coarse words or suspect actions, on the basis that if a person is generally well intentioned then the odd divergence from the straight and narrow will do no harm. But what Paul meant was that those whose thoughts are genuinely pure are the least likely to be tainted by obscenity, crudity or coarseness, whereas those who are habitually used to vulgarity will see in everything something that feeds their perverse perspective – as has happened with this phrase!

# Touch the hem of his garment

*And, behold, a woman, which was diseased with an issue of blood twelve years, came behind him, and touched the hem of his garment: for she said within herself, If I may but touch his garment, I shall be whole. But Jesus turned him about, and when he saw her, he said, Daughter, be of good comfort; thy faith hath made thee whole. And the woman was made whole from that hour.*

**Matthew 9:20–22**

*And when they were gone over, they came into the land of Gennesaret. And when the men of that place had knowledge of him, they sent out into all that country round about, and brought unto him all that were diseased; and besought him that they might only touch the hem of his garment: and as many as touched were made perfectly whole.*

Matthew 14:34–36

The hem of a garment clearly indicates the outer extremity of what a person is wearing, and those who attempted to touch this part of Jesus' clothes would have done so acting on the belief that their illness made them unworthy to come any closer to him – and found that even the extremities of such a great and influential person carried something of his power. So our modern phrase retains the expectation of being powerfully affected by entering even the outer sphere of influence (whether literal or figurative) of some influential or admirable personage.

## The tower of Babel

*And the whole earth was of one language, and of one speech. And it came to pass, as they journeyed from the east, that they found a plain in the land of Shinar; and they dwelt there. And they said one to another, Go to, let us make brick, and burn them throughly. And they had brick for stone, and slime had they for morter. And they said, Go to, let us build us a city and a tower, whose top may reach unto heaven; and let us make us a name, lest we be scattered abroad upon the face of the whole earth. And the* LORD *came down to see the city and the tower, which the children of men builded. And the* LORD *said, Behold, the people is one, and they have all one language; and this they begin to do: and now nothing will be restrained from them, which they have imagined to do. Go to, let us go down, and there confound their language, that they may not understand one another's speech. So the* LORD *scattered them abroad from thence upon the face of all the earth: and they left off to build the city. Therefore is the name of it called Babel; because the* LORD *did there confound the language of all the earth: and from thence did the* LORD *scatter them abroad upon the face of all the earth.*

**Genesis 11:1–9**

A *babel* is a noisy, confused situation. The name comes from the incredible tower built on the plain of Shinar. The people had decided to settle down in one place in defiance of God's instruction to populate the whole world. When God became aware of their actions, he scattered the people throughout the earth, and at the same time mixed up their languages so they couldn't properly understand each other. The Hebrew word *Babel* has a similar ring to the word *balal*, meaning 'confusion'.

## The tree of knowledge

*And out of the ground made the L*ORD *God to grow every tree that is pleasant to the sight, and good for food; the tree of life also in the midst of the garden, and the tree of knowledge of good and evil. 'But of the tree of the knowledge of good and evil, thou shalt not eat of it: for in the day that thou eatest thereof thou shalt surely die.'*

**Genesis 2:9, 17**

*And the woman said unto the serpent, We may eat of the fruit of the trees of the garden: but of the fruit of the tree which is in the midst of the garden, God hath said, Ye shall not eat of it, neither shall ye touch it, lest ye die. And the serpent said unto the woman, Ye shall not surely die: for God doth know that in the day ye eat thereof, then your eyes shall be opened, and ye shall be as gods, knowing good and evil. And when the woman saw that the tree was good for food, and that it was pleasant to the eyes, and a tree to be desired to make one wise, she took of the fruit thereof and did eat, and gave also unto her husband with her; and he did eat.*

**Genesis 3:2–6**

The *tree of the knowledge of good and evil* was the tree that stood in the Garden of Eden. The one prohibition that God placed upon Adam and Eve was eating its fruit. Hardly overburdened with long lists of do's and don'ts, the couple nonetheless failed to observe this restriction. As a consequence they were punished. Anyone talking of this particular tree today might be alluding to a situation in which someone has embarked upon a course of action that, as well as revealing valuable and hitherto hidden information, might also have disastrous consequences. In this sense it may be likened to the expression 'opening Pandora's box' derived from Greek myth. So we might say that the dropping of the first atomic bomb opened up a Pandora's box, or that it was like taking from the tree of the knowledge of good and evil.

## The tree of life

*And out of the ground made the LORD God to grow every tree that is pleasant to the sight, and good for food; the tree of life also in the midst of the garden, and the tree of knowledge of good and evil. 'But of the tree of the knowledge of good and evil, thou shalt not eat of it: for in the day that thou eatest thereof thou shalt surely die.'*

**Genesis 2:9, 17**

Genesis tells us that God planted a garden in the East, in Eden. In it he placed all kinds of trees, one of which was the tree of life. There was no specific command relating to this tree, although Adam and Eve were told they could not eat from the **tree of the knowledge of good and evil**. When they disobeyed this command, they forfeited the right of access to the tree of life and they were permanently banished from the garden. Finally, cherubim and a flashing sword were placed to protect the tree, in case Adam and Eve might have been tempted to return.

## Turn the other cheek

*But I say unto you, That ye resist not evil: but whosoever shall smite thee on thy right cheek, turn to him the other also.*

**Matthew 5:39**

When we *turn the other cheek* we deliberately do not respond to some act of unkindness, anger or violence with equivalent actions of our own. Instead we refuse to be drawn into an act of revenge, perhaps even – as Jesus urges here – going to the point of being prepared to submit to further ill treatment rather than lash out ourselves. This was a principle Jesus declared in the

Sermon on the Mount, where he sought to address the problem of people's inappropriate behaviour by highlighting the importance of correct thoughts and attitudes.

## The twinkling of an eye

*See* **In the twinkling of an eye**

# U

## Unicorn

*God brought them out of Egypt; he hath as it were the strength of an unicorn.*

Numbers 23:22

The *unicorn* is a creature of myth and legend. It is often seen in ancient texts or pictures and is portrayed as a noble horse-like creature with a solitary horn sticking up from its head. It is typically white and is often taken as a symbol of strength, courage and purity. The Bible too refers to a *unicorn*, but the animal it describes is believed to be a wild ox. As such, its primary feature was considered to be its prodigious strength, a concept taken up by Numbers 23:22. Although called *unicorn*, the creature could have more than one horn, as described in Deuteronomy 33:17 where it speaks of the 'horns of unicorns'.

# Unspotted from the world

*Pure religion and undefiled before God and the Father is this, To visit the fatherless and widows in their affliction, and to keep himself unspotted from the world.*

James 1:27

A person who keeps himself or herself *unspotted from the world* is someone who manages to maintain his or her purity despite the surrounding moral pollution. James mentions it as one half of true religion: on the one hand he encouraged his readers to offer practical help to orphans and widows, and at the same time he urged them to avoid those aspects of human behaviour that would corrupt and drag them away from their calling.

# V

## The valley of the shadow of death

*Yea, though I walk through the valley of the shadow of death, I will fear no evil: for thou art with me; thy rod and thy staff they comfort me.*

Psalm 23:4

The *valley of the shadow of death* is an expression that is used to describe the experience of going through particularly grim circumstances, such as a near-fatal illness or the unexpected death of a close relative or friend. The use of the word *shadow* gives the idea of a close encounter with mortality (though perhaps not the finality of death itself). It comes from one of the most loved passages in the Bible, Psalm 23, in which David describes how supported and protected he has felt by God even in those situations when there seemed to be little or no hope.

# A voice crying in the wilderness

*For this is he that was spoken of by the prophet Esaias, saying, The voice of one crying in the wilderness, Prepare ye the way of the Lord, make his paths straight.*

**Matthew 3:3**

*A voice crying in the wilderness* indicates someone whose message is largely ignored by others. Usually what that person says is a word of warning or caution, challenging people to think of the consequences of what they are doing or not doing. They are often regarded as cranks and misfits by the majority, who fail to hear anything salutary in what they say – or simply choose to dismiss it. Matthew, Mark and Luke saw John the Baptist as the fulfilment of this prophecy: his home was the desert and his message was less about himself than about urging people to get ready for the arrival of someone else. It was not surprising, therefore, that his activity reminded them of the words of the prophet Isaiah, spoken many years before. There may also be a hint of the way we use these words now, since John's ministry, though heeded by individuals, ultimately led to his death at the hands of Herod, who simply could not bring himself to act positively on what he heard.

# W

## The wages of sin (is death)

*For the wages of sin is death; but the gift of God is eternal life through Jesus Christ our Lord.*

Romans 6:23

The phrase *the wages of sin is death* is sometimes used to forecast or explain ill consequences from a particular act of wrongdoing. It comes from the apostle Paul's words in Romans where he directly links death to sin: if we continue to defy God, the outcome will be true death: eternal separation from him. If, however, we trust in God and depend on him and his grace, we will receive life, the gift of God through Jesus Christ.

## To wash your hands of something

*When Pilate saw that he could prevail nothing, but that rather a tumult was made, he took water, and washed his hands before the multitude, saying, I am innocent of the blood of this just person: see ye to it.*

Matthew 27:24

If I *wash my hands of something*, it doesn't mean that I physically clean them with soap and water. Instead, I choose to have nothing to do with what is going on, denying any responsibility in the matter. This was what Pilate did when the Jews were baying for Jesus' blood. He felt there was no case to answer and was caught between a desire not to see an innocent man suffer and a fear of potential unrest should the Jewish leaders not get their way. Unable to make a decision, he took a bowl of water and publicly washed his hands in it, declaring himself innocent of whatever might happen to Jesus.

## Watch and pray

*Watch and pray, that ye enter not into temptation: the spirit indeed is willing, but the flesh is weak.*

Matthew 26:41

If someone urges you to *watch and pray*, he or she is telling you to be spiritually alert. The words were origin-ally spoken by Jesus in the Garden of Gethsemane before his betrayal and arrest. His disciples had accompanied him and, doubtless because he was more aware than they of the impending storm of events that were about to overtake them all, he wanted them to be as vigilant as he was. Sadly, they were neither able to watch nor to pray, as tiredness repeatedly overcame them.

*See also* The **spirit is willing, but the flesh is weak**

## Wax

*In that he saith, A new covenant, he hath made the first old. Now that which decayeth and waxeth old is ready to vanish away.*

**Hebrews 8:13**

For most of us *wax* is what candles are made of, or a brownish substance that oozes out of our ears. In addition we might occasionally use the phrase *wax and wane*. The King James Version uses it many times in the latter sense and without the corollary, to mean 'grow' or 'become'. In the verse quoted from Hebrews the writer is describing something which is growing old.

## The weaker vessel

*Likewise, ye husbands, dwell with them according to knowledge, giving honour unto the wife, as unto the weaker vessel, and as being heirs together of the grace of life; that your prayers be not hindered.*

1 Peter 3:7

Long before the days of equal opportunities or feminism, Peter described wives as *the weaker vessel* of their husbands. In these more politically correct times the expression may have a broader meaning than that envisaged by the apostle. Today it can refer to anyone who is vulnerable in a given situation, perhaps less well suited to withstand the stresses and strains of events taking place. It should be noted that Peter used the term in the context of specifically requiring the husbands *not* to look down upon their wives, but to regard them with special respect and honour.

## Weighed in the balance and found wanting

*TEKEL; Thou art weighed in the balances, and art found wanting. PERES; Thy kingdom is divided, and given to the Medes and Persians.*

Daniel 5:27–28

If someone is given a position of responsibility within an organisation, government or business and then subsequently fails to match up to the necessary standards and expectations, then that person may be said to have been *weighed in the balance and found wanting*. In ancient Babylon, this was the charge laid against King Belshazzar, who had failed to learn the spiritual lesson of humility that his predecessor Nebuchadnezzar had. The consequence of this for the king was that his reign was almost immediately to come to an end through the invasion of the Medo-Persian Empire.

*See also* The **writing on the wall**

## What is truth?

*Pilate therefore said unto him, Art thou a king then? Jesus answered, Thou sayest that I am a king. To this end was I born, and for this cause came I into the world, that I should bear witness unto the truth. Every one that is of the truth heareth my voice. Pilate saith unto him, What is truth? And when he had said this, he went out again unto the Jews, and saith unto them, I find in him no fault at all.*

John 18:37–38

In the contemporary world, where the only absolute truth may appear to be that there is no such thing as absolute truth, Pilate's question, *What is truth?* may seem surprisingly up to date. He posed it in response to Jesus' claim that he was born to tell people the truth. Pilate's brief questioning of Jesus appeared to convince him that the case against him was pretty thin, and the passage tells us that he went and told his accusers that there was insufficient evidence against him.

## Whatever a man sows, that shall he reap

*Be not deceived; God is not mocked: for whatsoever a man soweth, that shall he also reap.*

Galatians 6:7

*But this I say, He which soweth sparingly shall reap also sparingly; and he which soweth bountifully shall reap also bountifully.*

2 Corinthians 9:6

A farmer knows perfectly well that if he sows wheat then, come harvest time, he will reap wheat. If he has sown another type of grain then he will, in turn, reap that. This expression, deeply rooted in the everyday agricultural world of the first century, means that a person will get back from any situation exactly what they have put into it. But see **Reap where you have not sown**

# Wheels within wheels

*The appearance of the wheels and their work was like unto the colour of a beryl: and they four had one likeness: and their appearance and their work was as it were a wheel in the middle of a wheel.*

Ezekiel 1:16

In the book of Ezekiel there is a description of living creatures depicting the glory of God that contains the expression, 'as it were *a wheel in the middle of a wheel.*' It is from this that we derive the phrase *wheels within wheels*. When we say this in everyday speech we are referring to the workings of a complex interrelated structure or organisation, the functioning of which appear mysterious and secretive to outsiders.

# Where two or three are gathered together

*For where two or three are gathered together in my name, there am I in the midst of them.*

Matthew 18:20

Sometimes if only a few people turn up for an event we might attempt to ward off discouragement by saying, *Where two or three are gathered together*. What we mean is that numbers are not what matters, because even with a small number there can still be a strong sense of purpose and direction. Jesus comforted his disciples here by saying that even though they might meet in small numbers, he himself would be present with them. With him as part of the gathering, there would be no need to feel disappointed or disillusioned.

## A whited sepulchre

*Woe unto you, scribes and Pharisees, hypocrites! for ye are like unto whited sepulchres, which indeed appear beautiful outward, but are within full of dead men's bones, and of all uncleanness.*

Matthew 23:27

A *whited sepulchre* is a dramatic way of calling someone a hypocrite, someone who says one thing and yet does another. Jesus here called the Pharisees, a prominent group of religious Jews, whited sepulchres. He was frequently at loggerheads with these men, who in many ways were respectable, earnest Jews to whom the masses looked for advice and example. Nevertheless, Jesus considered them to be hypocrites because their lives did not match up to their words, and they placed expectations upon the people that stifled, rather than encouraged, true faith. This dramatic description compares them to the

236

whitewashed tombs in which important people were buried: externally they looked fine and respectable, but inside they were dead and worthless.

## The widow's cruse

*Now there cried a certain woman of the wives of the sons of the prophets unto Elisha, saying, Thy servant my husband is dead; and thou knowest that thy servant did fear the LORD: and the creditor is come to take unto him my two sons to be bondmen. And Elisha said unto her, What shall I do for thee? tell me, what hast thou in the house? And she said, Thine handmaid hath not any thing in the house, save a pot of oil. Then he said, Go, borrow thee vessels abroad of all thy neighbours, even empty vessels; borrow not a few. And when thou art come in, thou shalt shut the door upon thee and upon thy sons, and shalt pour out into all those vessels, and thou shalt set aside that which is full. So she went from him, and shut the door upon her and upon her sons, who brought the vessels to her; and she poured out. And it came to pass, when the vessels were full, that she said unto her son, Bring me yet a vessel. And he said unto her, There is not a vessel more. And the oil stayed. Then she came and told the man of God. And he said, Go, sell the oil, and pay thy debt, and live thou and thy children of the rest.*

2 Kings 4:1–7

237

The *widow's cruse* does not refer to a relaxing sea holiday undertaken by a wife and paid for by her deceased husband's life insurance. Instead, it is used as a way of describing some seemingly insignificant quantity of an item, usually food or money, that never seems to run out. The phrase does not actually appear in the Bible, but comes from a story in 2 Kings where Elisha visited a poor widow. He asked her if she might provide him with food. She replied that she was preparing to eat the last of her supplies and then, she assumed, she would starve to death. He told her not to worry, but to go and prepare him a meal. He assured her that her cruse, or jug, of oil would never run out of liquid and so she and her son would survive the ravages of the famine that had swept the country. The story tells us that everything happened as Elisha had predicted. The lady made him a meal and subsequently found she always had enough for herself and her son to eat.

## The widow's mite

*And Jesus sat over against the treasury, and beheld how the people cast money into the treasury: and many that were rich cast in much. And there came a certain poor widow, and she threw in two mites, which make a farthing. And he called unto him his disciples, and saith unto them, Verily I*

*say unto you, That this poor widow hath cast more in, than*
*all they which have cast into the treasury: for all they did*
*cast in of their abundance; but she of her want did cast in*
*all that she had, even all her living.*

Mark 12:41–44

Mark records Jesus watching the comings and goings at the Temple treasury and says that he saw a poor widow toss a couple of small coins – mites – into the coffers. Although the amount was so small as to be insignificant against the larger gifts that had been casually thrown in by the rich, Jesus claimed that because the widow had given all she had, her generosity was far greater than that of the wealthy. The idea of *the widow's mite* has passed into the English language to mean a small gift of money that may nevertheless be as much or more than the giver can actually afford.

## The wind blows where it wills (lists)

*The wind bloweth where it listeth, and thou hearest the*
*sound thereof, but canst not tell whence it cometh, and*
*whither it goeth: so is every one that is born of the Spirit.*

John 3:8

In modern English the word *list* usually refers to that piece of paper we only discover we have left on the fridge door once safely arrived at the supermarket. It can also be used to describe a stricken ship that leans or lists to one side after a collision of some sort. From this latter meaning we can perhaps make the jump to Jesus' use of the word in this verse from John's Gospel. A ship leans where it wants to and from the context of what Jesus was saying it is clear that the word meant 'wills' or 'wants'. In other words, *the wind blows where it wills* (or *wants*). It is this that we mean when we use the expression to describe a situation over which we have no control, but which is simply in the hands of fate. In John chapter 3, Jesus is referring to the sovereign act of the spiritual new birth.

## The wings of a dove

*And I said, Oh that I had wings like a dove! for then would I fly away, and be at rest.*

Psalm 55:6

*Though ye have lien among the pots, yet shall ye be as the wings of a dove covered with silver, and her feathers with yellow gold.*

Psalm 68:13

Many people will know the phrase, *O for the wings, for the wings of a dove*. It comes from Felix Mendelssohn's anthem 'Hear my prayer', written in 1844 and often sung by choirs with the accompaniment of an organ. The piece is based on Psalm 55. The words are the expression of a desire to rid oneself of all the encumbrances and burdens of life and escape to a place of freedom and rest. It is not known precisely why the psalmist chose the dove, of all birds, to represent his flight, but it may have something to do with the dove being itself associated with the peace and harmony he desired.

## The wisdom of Solomon

1 Kings 3:16–27

A person who has the wisdom of Solomon is very fortunate. God appeared to this Old Testament king in a dream and promised to grant him one wish. The king asked for wisdom. In the Bible this quality is never an abstract, academic talent, but carries a sense of practical morality. Indeed, Solomon asked for wisdom so that he could rule his people and be able to judge them sensibly and fairly. His request was granted. He became the wisest person in the land, and today his wisdom has acquired a legendary status. One of his most notable rulings is recorded in 1 Kings 3. Two women came to him, both claiming motherhood over a solitary child. Having heard both sides of the story, Solomon ordered one of his servants to cut the boy in two. The real mother, rather than see her boy killed, pleaded for him to be handed over to her rival, while the latter was prepared to settle for half a child. By this clever trick Solomon rightly discerned who the child really belonged to, and ordered him to be handed to his rightful parent.

## Wise as serpents, and harmless as doves

*Behold, I send you forth as sheep in the midst of wolves: be ye therefore wise as serpents, and harmless as doves.*

Matthew 10:16

To *be as wise as a serpent, as harmless as a dove* is to walk a tightrope between two extremes. In the Bible the serpent is the archetypal creature of cunning, while the dove is a bird that threatens no other creature. Jesus, fully aware that he was sending his disciples out into an unforgiving, cynical and ruthless world, expected them to display extraordinary wisdom, and yet at the same time did not want it to be of the ruthless, manipulating type displayed by the serpent in the Garden of Eden: it was to be tempered by the innocence and purity of a peaceful dove.

# A wise/foolish virgin

Matthew 25:1–12

Jesus told a parable of ten virgins, each of whom had a lamp ready for the arrival of the bridegroom at a marriage. Five of them had sufficient oil, but five did not. When the groom arrived, very late, those without enough oil begged the others to give them some oil. They would not, so the five without were forced to go out and try to buy more oil. In their absence the door to the wedding feast was closed, and when they returned no amount of pleading could persuade those inside to open the door. From this story the two groups of virgins have sometimes been used to represent people who are wise and prepared for any circumstance and those who, for whatever reason, are foolish and are not so prepared.

# A wolf in sheep's clothing

*Beware of false prophets, which come to you in sheep's clothing, but inwardly they are ravening wolves.*

Matthew 7:15

Even in fairy tales there aren't many *wolves in sheep's clothing*. The closest may be the wolf in the grandmother's clothing in 'Little Red Riding Hood'. Nevertheless, the principle is exactly the same. *A wolf in sheep's clothing* is anyone who attempts to ingratiate themselves in a situation by pretending to be pleasant and harmless when the reality is that they are in fact a troublemaker. Their primary purpose for getting involved is to cause harm to those amongst whom they find themselves. Jesus used the expression to warn his followers to be on their guard against false prophets, people who, though apparently friendly and supportive, were actually intent on malicious and disruptive behaviour.

## The wolf shall lie down with the lamb

*See* The **lion shall lie down with the lamb**

## Word and deed

*See* In **word and deed**

## A word in season

*The Lord God hath given me the tongue of the learned, that I should know how to speak a word in season to him that is weary: he wakeneth morning by morning, he wakeneth mine ear to hear as the learned.*

Isaiah 50:4

*A word in season* indicates that ability to be able to say something appropriate, useful or challenging at just the right time. In Isaiah the sense is linked very much to the ability of the well-spoken word to encourage, support and restore those who are feeling tired and downtrodden.

## The writing on the wall

Daniel 5

*The writing is on the wall* does not refer to the levels of graffiti around our towns and villages thanks to an army of aerosol-canned youngsters who have turned vandalism into an art form. It refers to a much earlier instance of a similar thing, but with a far more portentous message. King Belshazzar of the Babylonians was feasting in his royal palace when a hand appeared and wrote the words, 'Mene, Mene, Tekel, Upharsin' on a wall. When the significance of the words was finally explained by Daniel, they were revealed as foretelling the demise of Belshazzar. In fact, that very night his city was captured and he himself was killed by the invading army of Darius the Mede. For that reason when we speak of the writing being on the wall, we mean that ominous signs seem to herald impending disaster.

*See also* **Weighed in the balance and found wanting**

# Y

## You of little faith
*See* O ye of little faith


## You reap what you sow
*See* Whatever a man sows, that shall he reap

# Appendix

## Phrases from the *Book of Common Prayer*

### And there is no health in us

Morning prayer, General Confession

The *Book of Common Prayer* contains sections on the visitation of the sick and a communion service for the sick. You might be tempted to expect that the words, *And there is no health in us* would appear in one or both of these places. This is not the case. They are part of the General Confession and describe not physical illness, but spiritual malaise. They are not necessarily intended to mean that the confessor is utterly wicked, but that just as a virus affects the whole of the body even though it may only manifest its symptoms in a specific way, so penitents recognise that they suffer from a spiritual sickness, and hence need God's healing.

## At death's door

*Their soul abhorred all manner of meat: and they were even hard at death's door.*

Psalm 107:18

The *Book of Common Prayer* uses Miles Coverdale's translation of the Psalms. He translated Psalm 107:18 as above. The King James Version has 'and they draw near unto the gates of death'. The use of the word 'near' in the King James Version neatly encapsulates the key element of the expression. Being *at death's door* describes those who are indeed close or near to death.

Other expressions from Coverdale's translation of the Psalter that have become part of the language include: **My cup shall be full**, from Psalm 23:5; **Flourish like a green bay-tree**, from Psalm 37:35; **The iron entered into his soul**, from Psalm 105:18; and **High-minded**, from Psalm 131:1.

# Dearly beloved, we are gathered together here in the sight of God, and in the face of this congregation

Solemnisation of Matrimony

These words are the opening ones in the Solemnisation of Matrimony. They are a reminder to all those present that what is taking place does so in two spheres: a heavenly one and an earthbound one. So well known is this phrase that it is often used when performing a caricature of a clergyman – doubtless armed with bucked teeth, starch-white dog collar and a quiver full of bland aphorisms to send all but the most resilient members of the congregation to sleep.

# Earth to earth, ashes to ashes, dust to dust

Burial of the dead

When a coffin is lowered to the ground at the burial service in a cemetery, the priest commits the body of the departed to the ground with the words, *Earth to earth, ashes to ashes, dust to dust*, and at the same time takes a small amount of earth and throws it on top of the coffin. Those who wish to sprinkle a small amount of earth often do so too. The words are a reminder of how the Bible sees the beginning of the human race, as Adam was moulded from the dust of earth and then God breathed life into him. At death, what was once a dynamic living and breathing human being now begins to decompose.

## Flourish like a green bay-tree

*See* **At death's door**

## From battle and murder, and from sudden death

The Litany

Written in more turbulent times than those we usually experience in the twenty-first century, the writers of the *Book of Common Prayer* faced death in an uncompromising manner. In the Litany, they wrote asking God to protect his people from *battle and murder, and from sudden death*. They had other concerns too which, though they seem only distant threats to us today, were far more significant threats in the life of everyday people four hundred years ago, such as lightning, tempest, plague, pestilence and famine.

# Have mercy upon us miserable sinners

## The Litany

According to the *Book of Common Prayer*, the Litany or General Supplication, is *to be sung or said after morning prayer upon Sundays, Wednesdays, and Fridays, and at other times when it shall be commanded by the Ordinary*. A litany is a prayer with invocations, each one being followed by the same response. The phrase *Have mercy upon us miserable sinners* comes in the opening lines of the Litany as well as in the repeated response.

# High-minded

*See* At death's door

# The iron entered into his soul

*See* At death's door

# Jews, Turks, Infidels and Hereticks

## Third Collect for Good Friday

Jews and Turks reading this may wonder why they have been singled out alongside the infidels and heretics. It hardly appears to be designed to help the cause of multi-culturalism. Whatever you might feel about those chosen for this small grouping to be found in the third collect for Good Friday, it must be said in defence that they are placed together in this way so that Christians might pray for God's mercy to fall upon them. It might also be good to remember that the words were originally penned in times several hundred years before political correct-ness arrived on the scene.

## My cup shall be full

*See* **At death's door**

## O all ye Works of the Lord, bless ye the Lord: praise him, and magnify him for ever

Benedicite, Omnia Opera

This phrase opens the canticle known as the *Benedicite, Omnia Opera*. It recalls part of the Apocrypha, the Prayer of Azariah and the Song of the Three Jews (which is one of the Additions to the Book of Daniel). It is a call to all the works of creation to praise God. It starts with the angels in heaven, then the heavens themselves, before moving on to the sun, moon and stars, vegetation, birds and animals. It concludes with an instruction to the singers themselves, Hananiah, Azariah and Mishael, to praise the Lord. At the end of each line the refrain 'praise him, and magnify him for ever' appears.

## O God, who art the author of peace and lover of concord

### Morning Prayer, Second Collect for Peace

When I was young and fascinated by the occasional plane that flew over the less crowded sky, there were two planes that always caused a stir at air shows: the symbolic Spit-fire and the sleek Concorde. I remember doing a project on the latter, so enthused was I by its shape and speed. What I could never understand was why God should be a lover of concord, as suggested by this phrase from the Second collect for peace. As I discovered later, what it really meant was that all true peace comes from God and therefore he loves concord, or as we might say today, harmony.

# An outward and visible sign of an inward and spiritual grace

Catechism

As part of their catechismal training prior to confirmation by a bishop, candidates have to explain the significance of the sacraments. They must explain what a sacrament is; the answer is that it is *an outward and visible sign of an inward and spiritual grace*. The questioning continues to show that for both sacraments (baptism and the Lord's Supper) there are two aspects. Each has an outward visible part and an inward spiritual part. Further questioning is conducted to show that the candidate has a grasp of these constituents in both sacraments.

# The pomps and vanity of this wicked world

Catechism

The Catechism in the *Book of Common Prayer* is 'an instruction to be learned of every person, before he be brought to be confirmed by the bishop'. The candidates have to answer a series of questions. One of these is 'What did your Godfathers and Godmothers then for you?' (at baptism). Part of the reply is that they renounced *the pomps and vanity of this wicked world*. The particular problem highlighted here is the false pretence and self-importance of so much of what humans do. In addition to this they will mention the works of the devil and the sinful lusts of the flesh, thereby covering the three areas the *Book of Common Prayer* highlights as being vehicles through which sin can ensnare a person.

## Read, mark, learn and inwardly digest

Collect for the second Sunday in Advent

At school our tyrannical Latin master used to take great pleasure in reciting these words to us whenever we had a new piece of work. Whether he was quoting them from knowledge of the *Book of Common Prayer* itself I cannot say, but he certainly was in keeping with their meaning. The collect for the second Sunday in Advent centres upon the appropriate attitude towards the Bible. It calls upon people to firstly read it, then make a note of what it says and finally (and perhaps most importantly) to internalise its teachings.

# Renounce the devil and all his works

## Baptism of infants

During the ceremony of infant baptism, also known as christening, the priest addresses the godfathers and godmothers explaining the nature of the promises they are about to make on behalf of the child. Having done this he or she then calls upon them to *renounce the devil and all his works*. As the Bible sees Satan behind the origin of all sin, the godparents are effectively being asked to turn away from all conceivable manner of wickedness.

# The Scripture moveth us in sundry places to acknowledge and confess our manifold sins

## Morning prayer

This phrase occurs at the beginning of *the Book of Common Prayer* and is uttered by the vicar or person leading the traditional service of morning prayer. It is part of the call to worship and reminds listeners of the many occasions when the Bible instructs its readers to bring their sins and failings to God. The *sundry places* are the specific instances within the pages of the Bible that encourage readers to avail themselves of the opportunity to do this.

# Therefore if any man can shew any just cause, why they may not lawfully be joined together, let him now speak, or else hereafter for ever hold his peace

## Solemnisation of Matrimony

Weddings are generally (or ought to be) noisy, cheerful affairs. Nevertheless within the marriage ceremony of the Church of England there is that moment when the whole congregation goes quiet and you can hear not only the church mouse, but the proverbial pin dropping. It comes when the person officiating says that if anyone of those present knows why the happy couple shouldn't get married they are to speak up, or shut up. Valid reasons are legal ones only, not the fact that 'the groom owes me a fiver' or 'the bride didn't give me a present for my last birthday'. A valid reason for interrupting a wedding at this point might be if it is known that one of the couple is already married.

# To have and to hold from this day forward, for better for worse, for richer for poorer, in sickness and in health, to love and to cherish, till death us do part

### Solemnisation of Matrimony

These words from the *Book of Common Prayer* encapsulate the teaching of Jesus in the New Testament, namely that from the beginning of time, God intended marriage to be an indissoluble partnership between one man and one woman. The language attempts to capture some of the extreme circumstances that might put pressure upon a couple as they walk through life together, and were doubtless included so that when those difficult times came they might remember the poetic force of the mutual promise they had made.

# To keep my hands from picking and stealing

### Catechism

One of the questions in the catechism asks, 'What is thy duty towards thy Neighbour?' The candidate should then reply with a long list, beginning with the command to love him 'as myself'. It then goes on to deal with areas such as submission to authorities, control of the tongue and other outward acts. Among these are included *to keep my hands from picking and stealing*. Quite what must not be picked is open to debate, but stealing appears to be fairly obvious.

# We have left undone those things which we ought to have done; and we have done those things which we ought not to have done

## Morning prayer, General Confession

This saying is not an apology for failing to do the buttons up on our shirt or for neglecting to shut a gate to a farmer's field when out for a country walk. What it acknowledges, rather, as part of the General Confession, is that there are sins of omission as well as sins of commission. Wrong can be just as much the absence of good deeds as the presence of bad ones. The Old Testament, in particular, repeatedly criticises the Israelites for their failure to stand up for the widows, orphans and strangers, as well as condemning more blatant wrong-doing such as theft, murder or adultery.

## Whose service is perfect freedom

Morning prayer, Second Collect for Peace

This apparently contradictory statement occurs in the second collect for peace. Collects are short prayers that usually come before the reading of the lesson in a Communion service. The word comes from the Medieval Latin *collecta* meaning 'prayer at an assembly'. What the phrase means is that to serve God, rather than being restrictive is, in actual fact, liberating.

## With this Ring I thee wed, with my body I thee worship, and with all my worldly goods I thee endow

Solemnisation of Matrimony

In the marriage service from the *Book of Common Prayer*, the bride and the groom make specific promises to each other. The man, when he gives the ring to his wife makes an additional promise. This consists of slipping a wedding ring on the fourth finger of his wife's hand, claiming that he will worship her with his body and then saying that everything he now has belongs to her as well. This is of considerable comfort to the woman, and if things go wrong will finance an army of divorce lawyers too.

# The world, the flesh and the devil

### The Litany

The phrase *the world, the flesh and the devil* is not actually found in the Bible. It comes, instead from the Litany in the *Book of Common Prayer*. The repeated phrase of this specific part of the Litany is 'Good Lord, deliver us'. The section is a prayer that takes up the theme of asking not to be led into temptation that comes from the Lord's Prayer. It is the fervent request to be rescued or not be found in a variety of difficult situations, both physical and spiritual. The phrase seeks to encapsulate the origins of sin that attack and disturb the Christian. They come from external influences (*the world*), internal ones (a person's own *flesh*, in the sense of 'sinful nature') and finally from *the devil*, Satan himself.